BEYOND THE LECTURE VOLUME 8

CONNOR WHITELEY

Any questions about the book, rights licensing, or to contact the author, please email connorwhiteley@connorwhiteley.net

DEDICATION

Thank you to all my readers without you I couldn't do what I love.

INTRODUCTION

I flat out love these Beyond The Lecture books, and I am so excited for another volume. For readers of past volumes, welcome back, it is great to see you again.

For new readers, the Clinical Psychology Reflections are back with a bang because this volume is filled with another 20 insightful, fascinating and thought-provoking reflections that are definitely going to improve your knowledge about clinical psychology and mental health.

From reflections on toxic living situations, to how psychologists are not empathy machines to the findings of a clinical psychology research conference that I attended, this volume is packed full of great information.

Moreover, clinical psychology is an amazing area of psychology. It can improve lives, transform them and save people for the better, and it can decrease psychological distress too. That's why I love this great area of psychology.

However, the problem with how clinical psychology is taught in lecture theatres and formal education is that there are only so many topics you can teach, only so many debates you can talk about and there is only so much research in the world so you cannot have lively, heated debates at university.

I wanted somewhere to address this issue.

Therefore, I decided to write these clinical psychology reflection books where I can use evidence and research and my own fact-based opinions to explore some of the hottest debates in clinical psychology. As well as explore other topics from a clinical psychology perspective.

All these books are extremely fun to write and are fascinating so I know you're going to enjoy them as well. Also, this has to be the best book in the series so far, because it explores topics in a lot more depth and we tackle some truly thought-provoking topics that impact the highest levels of clinical psychology practice and research.

If you're looking for an engaging, fascinating and easy-to-understand book exploring the edges of clinical psychology as well as other topics that you would never be taught at university, then this is the book for you.

You won't regret buying this book.

Who Am I?

Personally, I always love to know who the author is of the nonfiction I read so I know the information is coming from a good source. In case you're like me, I'm Connor Whiteley, the internationally bestselling author of over 60 psychology books.

In addition, I am the host of *The Psychology World Podcast,* a weekly show exploring a new psychology topic each week and delivering the latest psychology news. Available on all major podcast apps and YouTube.

Finally, I am a psychology graduate with a BSc (Hons) in Psychology With Clinical Psychology and a Placement year and an MSc in Clinical Psychology from the University of Kent, England.

So now we know more about each other, let's dive into some great clinical psychology reflections.

IS CLINICAL PSYCHOLOGY REALLY FOR YOU?

I really haven't wanted to write this reflection.

Normally, whenever I come up with an idea or I see something that has inspired me to write a reflection. I add it to my list and I write it as soon as possible but I have really struggled to start writing this next reflection, because it means I have to admit something that is going to completely change my desires, my dreams and my worldview.

I don't know if clinical psychology is what I want to do anymore.

I don't know if I want to become a clinical psychologist.

Let me explain what happened, because I firmly believe that a lot of aspiring psychologists will experience these feelings, they will seriously consider this and some people will be shocked I am even talking about this idea.

Recently, I've been reading the brilliant *Clinical Psychologist Collective* by Dr Marianne Trent. It's an engaging, insightful and brilliant collection of essays by over twenty clinical psychologists talking about how they got onto the clinical psychology doctorate. This allowed them to become fully qualified clinical psychologists.

Similar to what I have spoken about before on The Psychology World Podcast and in my other books, everyone's journey is unique, different and fascinating. One woman was talking about how she originally gave up on the doctorate and she spent a decade working, planning and executing drug and alcohol rehabilitation plans across the United Kingdom before she rejoined the doctorate and became a clinical psychologist.

Another person had the more standard route. She completed her psychology undergraduate degree, she built up her years of experience and then she applied a few times and got rejected before getting onto the doctorate.

Then there were lots of other people with other stories that fall in between those two ends of the spectrum.

However, I'm currently halfway through the book and I am really enjoying it, but I am realising certain patterns.

To be able to get onto the clinical psychology doctorate, as I have spoken a lot on the podcast and in my books before, you need a lot of clinical experience. You need to be volunteering, you need to be working and interacting with people with mental health conditions and you need to be privileged enough to be able to use your undergraduate degree to gain volunteering experience.

Equally, you really need to be an Assistant Psychologist to be able to get onto the doctorate. These are super competitive, super rare compared to the sheer demand of the jobs and I think the requirement of you being an Assistant Psychologist is stupid.

I have worked with Assistant Psychologists. They are amazing, brilliant and compassionate people. They are some of the loveliest people I know. Yet they don't actually do what a clinical psychologist does.

Assistant Psychologists are glorified notetakers in multidisciplinary teams, they don't deliver and they don't always support the delivery of psychological interventions. As well as clinical psychologists are mentors, supervisors, educators, advocates, and so much more than a therapist and researcher.

There are a million different jobs.

An assistant psychologist barely does a fraction of that, so how does taking notes silently in a meeting help me become a clinical psychologist?

In addition, the clinical psychology doctorate is super competitive and there will always be four or even five times as many applicants compared to the number of places, so unless you are so dedicated, psychology becomes your entire life and clinical psychology is your obsession. Then you probably won't get onto the doctorate.

Do you really want clinical psychology to become your entire life?

I'm not sure I do.

Why Couldn't I Do The Above?

Before I talk about the other reasons why I am starting to question my dedication to wanting to become a clinical psychologist, I want to reflect on the above from my personal point of view.

I mentioned you need a lot of volunteering experience both during your undergraduate and after your degree. During my undergraduate degree and my Masters, it was either COVID so it was impossible to get any experience, or my mental health was so bad that I couldn't interact with other people and I couldn't push myself. I was dealing with the results of being abused, hated and in fear for my life for a decade.

I was too scared, too shamed and too anxious to go outside and pursue volunteering experience.

In addition, it wasn't until the age of 21-years-old or thereabouts that I was actually able to drive. I couldn't get work experience or volunteering in mental health charities during my undergraduate degree because there wasn't much in Medway that I could get too, and the train is super expensive.

Then during my Masters, a massive chunk of my Masters was dealing with the fallout of my rape, my

Post-Traumatic Stress Disorder and recovery.

Furthermore, because my university was charging me an extra £2,000 because they were charging me full-time for a single term and then part-time for the rest of my degree. As well as I was living away from home to improve my mental health, my self-esteem and undo a decade of abuse, I had to pay rent, bills and food.

I could not afford to undertake volunteering or work experience.

I had to work a lot of Outreach just to survive and pay my bills. I didn't have time or money to do volunteering.

Furthermore, another reason why I didn't want or couldn't get volunteering or work experience is because I wanted to build up my author business, write books and start my podcast. I flat out love being an author, a business owner and a podcaster. If I became obsessed with clinical psychology, these amazing parts of my life wouldn't have happened.

I would be less happy if I didn't have writing, my business and my podcast in my life.

In terms of becoming a clinical psychologist, to some extent, this has left me in an extremely poor position. My lived experience, my books, my podcast and even my Outreach work where I have worked with children and young people for 6 years doing a very, very wide range of roles has left me with minimal clinical experience.

I have 3 days in a Gender Identity Clinic and 5

working days in a learning disability team. That is all the mental health experience I have. Besides all my own lived experience.

I will always keep applying for mental health jobs, assistant psychologist roles and more in an effort to pursue clinical psychology but I know there will always be more people with more experience than me. Because they were able to pursue clinical psychology experience and volunteering earlier in their journey.

What's Your Dream and Values and What Do You Really Want?

I want to help people.

The event that really made me start thinking about my commitment to clinical psychology was the start of a business course that commenced about four weeks ago. The first assignment of the course for professional writers was write down your dream.

This is what I wrote:

My dream is to be a part-time indie author and a part-time clinical psychologist. I flat out love writing, publishing, podcasting and everything related to CGD Publishing. I couldn't live without it and creating and being a business owner brings me a lot of joy and happiness. It just makes life more fun.

However, my creative voice feeds off interacting with the real world. My creative voice uses situations, people and everyday interactions in different ways in my fiction and nonfiction. It is by interacting and living in the real world that I learn what's happening beyond my social world and that can be immensely valuable in my stories. Also, I flat out love psychology, it forms the nonfiction branch of CGD Publishing. And I want to be a clinical psychologist so I can improve lives, help others and put my BSc and MSc into practice, and it will keep me learning.

I love learning. Be it about mental health, psychology, writing, business and on and on and on.

Also, being a part-time clinical psychologist would mean it takes pressure off the writing and business "having" to earn so much money so I can live and enjoy my life.

As long as I keep the writing fun that is all that matters.

Finally, in terms of money, I want to earn at least £50,000 a year but I can honestly see myself earning way, way beyond that. Yet £50,000 is a great amount to live on in the UK and it would be the minimum that I want to earn year on year.

Nonetheless, if you really think about what I wrote you could change clinical psychologist out very easily. What my dream actually is when it comes to being a clinical psychologist is:

- Helping people
- Interacting with the real world
- Live in the real world
- Help others
- Improve lives
- Put my BSc and MSc into practise
- Keep me learning

Honestly, in my life that is all I want and you don't need clinical psychology to do any of them.

Ticking off all those things would make me happy, smile and really pleased with my life. As long as I can tick those boxes and be a part-time writer and podcaster, I will be happy in terms of my work.

There are other, less-competitive routes that will still make me happy.

In addition, here's a quote from page 139 of The Clinical Psychologist Collective: *In Clinical Psychology, you incorporate many different job roles together; you are at once a clinician, a therapist, an advocate, a leader, a trainer, a supervisor of others, a mentor, a mental health specialist, a researcher and a policy writer.*

There's more mentioned in that important paragraph but I can make my point with that quote. When I consider my aim in life is to help people, improve lives and decrease psychological distress, do I really need to do all those other roles to complete my aims?

No.

To be able to help people, I could do the following jobs instead:

- CBT Therapist
- Psychological Wellbeing Practitioner
- Counsellor
- Mental health support worker
- Family worker
- Social worker
- Mental health nurse
- Health psychologist

- Therapist
- Clinical health psychologist
- Forensic psychologist
- Educational psychologist
- Counselling psychologist

And a million other jobs

Ultimately, at the end of this reflection, I want you to know that if you want to become a clinical psychologist, that is amazing. That is brilliant and you are incredible for wanting that. Yet you have to realise, be aware of and understand that it is a difficult road to go down.

And after everything my rape, my child abuse, my anorexia and all the different social, economic and other reasons that have prevented me from getting work experience or volunteering and when I consider what makes me truly happy. I am starting to doubt if clinical psychology is for me.

There are a thousand other important, valid and still-hard paths that I could go down that would make me happy, but they don't involve clinical psychology.

Here are some questions to get you thinking at the end of this reflection:

- How many personal stories have you read or listened to about how people got onto the clinical psychology doctorate?
- How much mental health work experience or volunteering experience have you got?

- Have you made a plan on how to get more?
- What are you prepared to sacrifice for your dream of becoming a clinical psychologist?
- What's your why?
- What would make you truly happy in your working life?
- Could your why and what makes you truly happy be found in other mental health jobs that doesn't involve becoming a clinical psychologist?

These will be really hard questions and like me, at first, you will probably bend the truth. Yet I strongly, strongly suggest you sit down and give these questions a long, honest think and write down your answers.

They might surprise you, shock you and put you on a brand-new path in life.

And in the end, you might find something far more rewarding than you ever thought possible.

HOW COULD SINGLE SESSION THERAPY BE USED IN MENTAL HEALTH SERVICES?

Personally, it's very rare for me to be randomly writing an episode of The Psychology World Podcast and then suddenly, it takes a massive reflective turn. That's what happened in the episode *What is Single Session Therapy*.

In that podcast episode, I was writing along, giving listeners and readers all the information and then I realised in the real-world, at least in the United Kingdom, you couldn't apply this knowledge very easily. Therefore, I really focused on reflecting about single session therapy, how we could use it to improve mental health services in the UK and some of the challenges that we could face in implementing this stark, but powerful, change.

Below is the very thought-provoking, useful and

insightful psychology article that the episode was based on.

I hope you enjoy it as much as I did writing it.

***

After subscribing to a few Continued Professional Development newsletters and seeing the option for Single Session Therapy on my university's counselling form, I finally decided it was time to investigate this type of psychotherapy in more detail. Traditionally, we know that psychological therapy can take months of therapy sessions to be fully effective and to improve a client's life for the better. Yet some therapists and researchers argue that a single session of psychological therapy is more than enough for some clients.

Therefore, in this clinical psychology podcast episode, you'll learn what is single session therapy, what is the evidence base for single session therapy and how might Single Session Therapy be used in the future.

What Is Single Session Therapy?

The main, basic principle behind Single Session Therapy is that a single session of psychological therapy might be more than enough to support clients with their mental health difficulties. Also, this isn't a theoretical model nor is it a standalone psychological approach, like cognitive behavioural therapy. Instead Single Session Therapy is a framework that helps therapists to conduct their therapy sessions in a way that maximises the efficacy of every session regardless of the type of therapy.

Personally, I think this is an interesting idea because whilst it wouldn't work for a wide range of mental health conditions. For example, you cannot undo or treat someone's depression, anxiety, Post-Traumatic Stress Disorder amongst other mental health conditions in a single therapy session. You might be able to support people with subclinical conditions just enough so their mental health difficulties don't become more severe where they need longer-term, more expensive psychological support for a longer period of time.

That's actually a really interesting idea. Maybe offering people a single session as a preventative measure so they don't need to get so severe that they need to be put on a waiting list for longer-term therapy for years.

Furthermore. Single Session Therapy isn't actually about therapy only lasting a single session. Hoyt and Talmon (2014b) argue that one of the massive misconceptions people have about Single Session Therapy is that it means a client only has a single treatment session.

In my opinion, I would add if you didn't want people to have that misconception, then don't include "single session" in the name. To me, that's common sense but I didn't name it.

Moreover, this misconception comes from the main idea behind Single Session Therapy. The basic idea is that a therapist works with a client to make sure they get the most out of every session of the therapy with the idea that every single session can potentially be the last one. Maybe this is because of dropout, poor treatment adherence, clients not being ready to start therapy, clients not having the right therapist for them at that moment in time or clients not having a capacity to change at that moment in time.

Interestingly, according to Hoyt and Talmon (2014b), the most common number of therapy sessions a client has is 1. I think that's fascinating because it shows that if most clients do only have a single session then as aspiring and qualified psychologists, we need to move heaven and earth to make sure the client gets the most out of this session. Even if the client never comes back, I would prefer to give my future clients as much knowledge, techniques and support as possible so if they never return. They might be okay in the future, or slightly better off than they would have been otherwise.

Is Single Session Therapy Enough for Some People?

In my opinion, as someone who has experienced depression, anxiety, post-traumatic stress disorder, anorexia and a bunch of other mental health conditions because of child abuse and rape. I know Single Session Therapy would not be a good fit for me and this would not have been useful in the slightest, but for some people a single session of therapy is enough.

Interestingly, when Talmon (1986) noticed a high

dropout rate in the psychotherapy service he was working in, he investigated why there was a high dropout and he found that 78% of clients said they had benefited from a single session of therapy so they didn't feel like they needed to return.

Additionally, this idea was later confirmed by Hoyt who conducted the first study into Single Session Therapy and out of 60 clients, 58% of them believed they didn't need additional therapy sessions after their first session. As well as these findings have been confirmed in additional research studies all over the world.

Nonetheless, my issue with Single Session Therapy is it is clear that there is strong potential for Single Session Therapy, especially as a preventative measure. Yet how do we apply this knowledge to the real world? In the United Kingdom, to be able to access psychological support, you essentially need to have two believable suicide attempts otherwise you cannot access therapy. That is how bad and how high the mental health criteria is for public sector mental health support, and this is the biggest employer of psychologists in the United Kingdom.

How Could Single Session Therapy Fit into The Public Sector?

I spoke about this in my book, Clinical Psychology Reflections Volume 6, with the Lanson Model in Cornwall. If there is a clinical psychologist in doctors and in primary healthcare then there is a chance, you might be able to book one session of therapy with a psychologist and hopefully that would be enough to help you decrease your psychological distress, and if you needed more then you would be put on the waiting list for longer-term support.

However, in my experience, as a rape survivor, I know sexual trauma is on the more extreme end of mental health conditions. Yet if I went for a single session of therapy, I started to feel hopeful about the future and then I was put on a public sector waiting list for years that alone would make my mental health worse.

There are no good solutions.

Conclusion

At the end of this podcast episode, whilst I have doubts because of my own mental health experiences about the usefulness of Single Session Therapy in the real world. I strongly believe we should be looking into offering clients one therapy session in primary healthcare to act as a preventative measure. This means there is a good chance people's mental health might not continue to decline to the point where they have clinically significant levels of distress that meet the criteria for different mental health diagnoses and then they need to be put on waiting lists for years.

Our waiting lists for psychological therapies are extremely long, they need to be reduced and the way to reduce the waiting lists is to reduce the need for them in the first place. If we can stop people's mental health from declining by giving them the therapeutic skills, techniques and self-advocacy to manage their mental health before they get severe enough to need longer-term therapy. Then this could benefit our mental health services in multiple ways. It means we could focus our extremely limited resources on the individuals with the most severe mental health needs, we could give mental health support to everyone regardless of whether they have two believable suicide attempts or not and so on.

Single Session Therapy might not be for everyone, but it might be a game changer in primary mental healthcare if we somehow manage to find the funding, implement it and find mental health services willing and able to trial it out.

And that's the hard part. Mental health services are already stretched to breaking point and many will not have the resources to trial this brand-new approach without additional funding and staff.

The odds might always be against new ideas, but that's why we always need to be trying, testing and finding new solutions to old problems.

What do you think?

Clinical Psychology References and Further Reading

Bertuzzi, V., Fratini, G., Tarquinio, C., Cannistra, F., Granese, V., Giusti, E. M., ... & Pietrabissa, G. (2021). Single-session therapy by appointment for the treatment of anxiety disorders in youth and adults: a systematic review of the literature. *Frontiers in Psychology*, *12*, 721382.

Campbell, A. (2012). Single-session approaches to therapy: Time to review. *Australian and New Zealand*

Journal of Family Therapy, *33*(1), 15-26.

Hoyt, M.F. & Talmon, M. (2014b). Editors' Introduction: Single Session Therapy and Walk-In Services. In M.F. Hoyt & M. Talmon (eds.) (2014a), op. cit., pp. 2-26.

Hoyt, M.F. & Talmon, M. (eds.) (2014a). Capturing the Moment. Single Session Therapy and Walk-In Services. Bancyfelin, UK: Crown House.

Hoyt, M.F., Talmon, M. & Rosenbaum, R. (1990). Sixty attemps for planned single session therapy, manoscritto non pubblicato.

Hymmen, P., Stalker, C. A., & Cait, C. A. (2013). The case for single-session therapy: Does the empirical evidence support the increased prevalence of this service delivery model?. *Journal of Mental Health*, *22*(1), 60-71.

Kim, J., Ryu, N., & Chibanda, D. (2023). Effectiveness of single-session therapy for adult common mental disorders: a systematic review. *BMC psychology*, *11*(1), 373.

Slive, A., McElheran, N., & Lawson, A. (2008). How brief does it get? Walk-in single session therapy. *Journal of Systemic therapies*, *27*(4), 5-22.

Talmon, M. (1990). Single Session Therapy. San Francisco: Jossey-Bass (Tr. it. Psicoterapia a seduta singola. Milano: Erickson).

Weir, S., Wills, M., Young, J. & Perlesz, A. (2008). The implementation of Single Session Work in community healt. Brunswick, Australia: The Bouverie Centre, La Trobe University.

Young, J., Weir, S., & Rycroft, P. (2012). Implementing single session therapy. *Australian and New Zealand Journal of Family Therapy*, *33*(1), 84-97.

DON'T WAIT, DEAREST PSYCHOLOGIST

At the moment, I'm close to finishing Miranda Hart's new book *I Haven't Been Entirely Honest With You.* I highly recommend the book for aspiring and qualified psychologists because it takes you through her journey of healing and recovering from chronic illness. Yet it is basically a psychology book and it focuses on how our learnt behaviours, lack of self-compassion and kindness and a bunch of other psychological concepts impact our physical health.

And Miranda Hart is just brilliant too.

Anyway, in the last fifty-ish pages of the book, there is a very powerful section that I really like. It focuses on the idea of *don't wait.* As this isn't too much of the book and there are a million little gemstones in the book, it counts as fair use if I include the following chunk:

"Make the best of where you are. Life is not about outcomes. Cease assessing and evaluating. Let it all unfold. Life isn't linear. However we feel, however it seems, we are always in progress.

Don't wait until you are ready.

Don't wait until you are fixed to start a relationship.

Don't wait until you are thinner or fatter to wear that dress.

Don't wait until you are better to find meaning.

Don't wait until you are confident to start working on a project.

Don't wait until you feel worthy to forge friendships.

Don't wait until you feel brave.

You will receive courage and worth if you start. Believe, then move out to receive."

Personally, as a rape survivor, this has a lot of different meanings and it is important to understand in the trauma context. Yet this can be applied to aspiring and qualified psychologists in a lot of different ways too.

This first example is a joke but I am sure that it will still be true for a lot of different students and qualified psychologists. Yet don't wait to start your dissertation or your research paper or any other of the hundreds of projects we all naturally put on the back burner because we are waiting for the right moment, the right amount of energy and for the right time where our workload is a little less.

That time or any one of those "rights" will probably never come dear psychologist. So please, don't wait, don't hesitate, try chipping away at that massive project because you might find that it is awful and hard and long. Yet so worth it in the end. Or you might be like me and you start it, love it and you wonder why you resisted the project for so long.

Secondly, don't wait to start the next step or chapter in your psychology journey. You might be waiting until you've learnt about a particular topic before you apply for some work experience, you might be waiting another year until you apply for the clinical psychology doctorate or that new role that you really want to do but you don't feel ready for.

There will always be excuses or more things that you could do to "better" prepare yourself for the next stage of your psychology chapter. Maybe if we all lived another thousand years, we really could go slowly and make sure we do everything "carefully" and "right". Yet we don't live in that sort of world, and I am grateful for that.

Even if you don't meet all the criteria for a job, apply for it. If you are passionate, excited and you really want to learn from a particular job or person, then apply, write to them and just try.

Don't wait, dear psychologist.

What's the worst that can happen?

The worst that can happen to you is very simple. The organisation or the person that you've written or applied to, might simply say no. That's okay. That's great. At least you tried. Think about all the wannabe clinical psychologists that are just waiting to be brave enough, just waiting to have the "perfect" resume and just waiting until the magical stars align so they're guaranteed to get it.

The world really doesn't work like that.

Thirdly, if we step away from academics and psychology jobs for a moment, let's look at our social connections and our friends and potential dates and partners. As Miranda said in her book, don't wait to forge that friendship, don't wait to ask that person out and certainly don't wait for that person to ask you out because, they might be nervous, anxious or shy. They might not think that you're interested in them and you two might go your entire lives without asking or acting on your feelings.

By waiting, you're denying yourself a chance at happiness, wonder and delight. If you wait, you might miss out on all on those happy memories and chances of connections. All those walks, or conversations or holidays together that you might have loved if only you asked them out.

Don't wait, dear psychologist.

Don't wait for anyone.

This applies to friendships. If you want to be friends with someone because they're interesting, they're cool or you get on great at university or work and you want a deeper friendship with them. Don't wait. Start talking to them, inviting them out and start creating that deeper friendship over time because you never know where it's going to lead you.

It might lead to nothing, but if you wait, if you delay, if you don't put yourself first then you will definitely miss out on what might have been.

All those great days or nights out, all those fun, deeper conversations and all those amazing laughs that our friends give us.

Don't wait, dearest psychologist.

Finally, if you have a chronic illness or mental health difficulty then you might be tempted to hide away from the world. You might be waiting until your physical or mental health is so much better before you start taking steps towards being a clinical psychologist. You might want to wait another year or two or five before you go to university, before you apply for that mental health volunteering, or you might be waiting for another million things to fall into place first of all before you get started.

I know the feeling.

During the worst of my mental health because of my rape, I didn't want to take steps towards becoming a clinical psychologist. I physically and mentally couldn't and I was too depressed, too suicidal and there were plenty of days when I couldn't get out of bed.

Then when I was struggling with my anorexia, this only happened even harder because I was always dealing with something.

However, after I achieved most of my recovery and when my anorexic self was still powerful but wasn't making me quite as ill as it was, I decided, I didn't want to wait anymore. I didn't want to hesitate and I wasn't "fixed" 100% and there were still days when my mental health just died, but I didn't want to wait anymore.

I focused back on my clinical psychology journey and some of the steps were really small, so small that some people might argue that they were meaningless but they weren't to me. And it was still a step towards becoming a clinical psychologist.

So even if you have a chronic physical health and mental health condition as impossible as it seems at times, don't wait to become a clinical psychologist.

One tiny step forward is better than no step at all. Even reading one article on how someone became a clinical psychologist a week is better than nothing.

The world is yours for the taking if only you act, go forward and do things without hesitation.

Don't wait, or you miss losing out on a lot of amazing things that might have happened if only you were brave, if only you were x, y and z.

Never wait.

DO CLINICAL PSYCHOLOGISTS IN PRIVATE PRACTICE NEED A THERAPEUTIC WILL?

A few days ago, I was listening to an episode of The Aspiring Psychologist Podcast and the interview guest was talking about her thesis research on fear of death and terror management theory. And towards the end of the podcast episode, there was a single idea that I flat out loved, and that's the focus of this reflection.

The idea is that clinical psychologists in private practice might need therapeutic wills in case they die when they're a practising clinical psychologist or another form of mental health professional.

The reason for therapeutic wills is that as a buffer against the fear of death, we make wills for ourselves. This allows us to control our finances, our estate, our possessions and so on. This allows us to control who gets what, what charities and organisations can benefit from our death and so on.

Wills allow us to create a legacy for ourselves after we die, so we can die knowing this is not the end, and our impact on the world will continue. It is the same thinking behind our legacy through having children amongst other buffers against death anxiety.

Now, I'm limiting the need of therapeutic wills to private practice because as much as this potentially sounds bad. If you're working in the public sector and you die, your workload will simply be passed off to someone else. You, as the deceased, have no input or control over who clients see after you're no longer about.

Very similar to how if you leave a mental health service, then your caseload is simply passed to someone else.

Therefore, in the rest of this reflection, I'll reflect on the need for therapeutic wills and what are some of the important aspects to do with this practice.

What Is Terror Management Theory?

Below is an extract from an episode of The Psychology World Podcast called What Terror Management Theory Can Teach Us About Christmas.

"Leading us onto Terror Management Theory, which is a branch of psychology research that was developed in 2015 with Jeff Greenberg, Tom Pyszczynski and Sheldon Solomon writing their book *The Worm at the Core* which is all about death anxiety. With the book proposing that death anxiety drives people to adopt a worldview that both defends as well as defends them from facing reality. Since the theory proposes that when thoughts about death are in our awareness, we attempt to remove these thoughts by suppressing them, engaging in behaviour that reduces our sense of vulnerability or we deny the threat exists.

In addition, Terror Management Theory suggests that a lot of our own life decisions are, in reality, distractions to help us deal with our own death anxiety. In other words, the concerns and worries that a person has about their own death, someone else's or the process of dying itself.

And I realise now that when I thought of doing this podcast episode, I thought it would be really cheery but now I realise how much I'm talking about death. But I promise you it will get more cheery soon.

Anyway, life choices like our careers, rituals and our routines are all ways that allow us to give meaning and purpose to our lives and this allows us to believe that we play an important role in the world. Yet according to the theory, these are only distractions from our death anxiety and the truth is that we live in a meaningless way."

If you want to learn more about that episode then this fascinating episode and the rest of the backlist of The Psychology World Podcast is available on all major Podcast apps and YouTube.

Are Therapeutic Wills Needed?

Ultimately, I think yes, therapeutic wills are definitely needed because all of us aspiring or qualified mental health professionals get into mental health work because we want to help people. We want individuals with mental health difficulties to thrive, decrease their psychological distress and improve their lives.

If we die unfortunately, all of a sudden, then I would rather die knowing that my clients had some support waiting for them. whether, this is a mental health service, another psychotherapist or counsellor that I trust to look after my clients or a booklet that someone gives them.

I just want my future clients to have some kind of support in case I die. And I suppose this sort of touches on the framework of Single Session Therapy. It's something I'm starting to look at for an episode of The Psychology World Podcast, but I don't know too much about it at the moment.

What I do know is that it's the idea that mental health professionals approach the session as if this is the only one. Of course, it is not good for every mental health condition, and this would be rubbish for me because of my complex trauma background but it is an interesting idea.

Maybe, sometimes, we need to approach sessions in private practice like they are the only ones in case we do die all of a sudden.

On the other hand, I just find that a very scary, anxiety-provoking and just terrifying idea, but maybe strike a balance. I always like to live in the moment where I can and I enjoy every moment of life in case I die the next day.

Yet it is difficult.

Moreover, as a client, I would have no idea what the hell would happen if any of my three counsellors had died during my counselling. I would have been distressed, concerned and perhaps a little hopeless. Especially, if my specialist rape counsellor had died all of a sudden. She was amazing, she really helped me and I would have been devastated if our work had ended early.

In that case, I would have been transferred to another counsellor in the rape service, but for my child abuse and my anorexia counselling. I would have nowhere else to go, and these were private counsellors didn't have anyone to check in with besides supervision.

Maybe supervision and clinical supervisors should have a say in what happens to a caseload after a counsellor has died. Yet that isn't the job of supervision and ultimately, that would require the sharing of personal and client details so once the counsellor dies, the supervisor can contact them.

That is an ethical nightmare and possibly legal nightmare too.

Personally, as an aspiring psychologist, if I just throw my two pennies out there and say we live in a fantasy world where I don't need to think about ethical rules or legal implications. I would like to have another trusted mental health professional in my therapeutic will who would get my clients after I died.

Afterwards, it would be up to the other professional if they are the best person to see the client or whether the other professional should signpost them elsewhere.

However, this is still not perfect because, what about my notes? What about the other professional's emotions and grief about my death? if I was close enough to want to leave my clients to them, we must have been close and I seriously trusted them?

Would they be in a fit state to support my clients?

This is before we even think about clinical notes. The majority of mental health professionals create short-hand or coded notes so they're next to useless without them, so would the other mental health professional even understand what the client was going through with me?

Probably not.

Ultimately, whilst the idea of therapeutic wills is not commonplace and I don't think this is going to change anytime soon. Yet I do believe that this is a good thought exercise. It isn't a happy one because no one likes to think about death but we should have from time to time. And there will always be a legal and ethical maze round the idea of therapeutic wills, I still think they are useful to consider.

What would your therapeutic will include?

I'm curious.

NEVER FORGET HOW PHYSICAL HEALTH IMPACTS MENTAL HEALTH AND VICE VERSA AND CONSIDERING WORKING IN A NEW AREA

There are times when something happens in our personal lives that have such a subtle but massive impact on us, as aspiring or qualified psychologists, that it has the potential to change our careers. At the time, it might not seem like it but the lessons we take away from a given event might eat away at us until we reflect and look at them in depth.

That's what I'm going through at the moment with my focus on how chronic illness impacts mental health.

In this reflection, you'll learn how chronic illness can impact mental health and vice versa, how clinical psychologists can work in this area and why I am considering working in this area. Not in that order but by the end of this reflection, you'll have a much better understanding of these topics.

Why Am I Talking About Chronic Illness and Mental Health?

I've always known about my partner's chronic health issues and it's always been a part of our casual relationship. It was why it was so difficult for us to actually schedule in our first date because they were either working a lot on coursework (their unmedicated ADHD is a barrier for them) or they were bedbound because of their health issues.

This has led them to cancel a few of our dates and hangouts together, because their chronic illness had knocked them out amongst other issues.

When this happens, I allow myself to feel the emotions of being sad and disappointed that we couldn't hang out. I don't judge my thoughts or try to stop them so I let them pass without judgment. Then I feel better and crack on with my day.

However, two days ago, there was a small, subtle event that I hope I never forget. It is subtle and a lot of people would say meaningless but as an aspiring psychologist, it was important to me.

To set the scene, me and my partner both play Dungeons and Dragons with our other friends. We are the "evil" characters in the party (I reject the notion) and it was a lot of fun hanging out, laughing and plotting together. The fantasy party was a lot of fun too and it was such a lovely afternoon.

Our characters even got arrested for trying to

steal a royal baby to save hundreds of innocent lives.

He was going to go to a good home I promise, I checked!

Anyway, this isn't a moral philosophy book and I repeat, I did not do anything. So me and my partner had a great time together and at dinner, we spoke for hours about our exams, our Easter breaks, Demonslayer because I finished the manga and on and on and on.

What I really like about us getting together is we talk about literally everything under the sun without any silence.

We were originally going to go back to our friend's house for a Eurovision party with the rest of the Dungeons and Dragons lot, but the house was small, there wasn't enough space for us and I noticed my partner was a little off. Not with me but they were hurting more than normal and they started to seem less engaged with everyone else.

I didn't think anything of it.

Until I was driving my partner back to their university accommodation and they mentioned have I ever heard of anhedonia. Of course, I had because it's the technical term for "loss of interest" commonly seen in depression but I'm dyslexic and I don't do sounds very well, so I didn't realise. We had a conversation about that, I mentioned it's common in depression and my partner said that they aren't depressed, their physical health just gets them down.

We were talking for ages afterwards and they

mentioned how as a kid they had so much energy, they could do so much and they didn't have any health problems. Come puberty, they couldn't do so much, they were bedbound a lot of the time and they hate it.

They hate how they can't go out with their friends much because they are normally too ill, when they want to go clubbing no one is about or one of their hips or another joint is messed up. And so on.

Just not being able to do anything makes them depressed at times. Sometimes they're so depressed because they're in constant pain that they can't get out of bed.

Finally for this section, it all led to a conversation over text today about how my partner just doesn't think it's fair on me for us planning to hang out, but their health is always too bad for them to leave their room. Even coming to Dungeons and Dragons is hard enough some days once a week.

I told them I care about them, if they need anything they should text me and so on.

Never Forget Physical Health Impacts Mental Health and Vice Versa

I wanted to tell you all this because sometimes as aspiring and qualified psychologists we can forget that our physical health can impact our mental health. Thankfully, a lot of us will never know what living with a chronic illness is like but for those that do live with a chronic condition, it is awful and very life-limiting.

They cannot get the same life satisfaction, quality of life and they cannot do the same activities that we take for granted. This is important to remember because often as psychologists we focus on early experience, rules to live by, feelings, thoughts, behaviours and emotions. I am just naming boxes off Beck's Cognitive Model of Depression, and we don't always think about physical health.

I do acknowledge that the biggest reason for this is because psychology is so well protected that if someone did have a physical condition. They would be seen by thousands (it feels like) medical professionals first before they would ever see a psychologist.

This means that people with physical conditions don't always get to psychological professionals even if they need it.

Personally, I don't always think this is a bad idea, medical services do a lot worse things in my opinion, because if the medical condition can be seen too and its impact on an individual's quality of life reduced. This is a good thing and hopefully, this will have a knock-on effect on improving the client's mental health too.

My partner earlier mentioned how they'll be fine as soon as they get some medication to cover up their symptoms. I think this is how it works for a lot of clients, once they get some kind of medication to manage their physical condition so their quality of life and life satisfaction can improve then their mental health improves too.

Nonetheless, there are two more areas we need to think about in this intersection between physical and mental health. What about people whilst they're waiting for their medical condition to be discovered and a medication found?

My partner doesn't know what's medically wrong with them and because it is so hard to get a doctor's appointment in the United Kingdom at the time of writing (May 2025), they will be waiting until Mid-June at the earliest. A referral to a specialist will likely be another 6-months and so on.

What will happen to my partner's mental health in the meantime?

Personally, I don't want to think about it as their partner but as an aspiring psychologist, I know it will probably continue to decline. Especially, if their health continues to decline like it has over the past few months. Thankfully, they have their support system in place and they seem upbeat about their health if not annoyed that this is happening in the first place.

They've been dealing with their poor health their entire life, so I suppose they've got coping mechanisms in place.

Nonetheless, as aspiring and qualified psychologists, we need to remember that sometimes we might need to provide psychological support to individuals with chronic illnesses who are waiting a diagnosis and medication to help improve their lives.

Psychologists working in this area can help with pain management, negative self-talk and several other areas of physical health.

A final area of this physical and mental health topic I want to talk about is, what about the people who don't have a medical solution to their chronic condition?

One of my friends has chronic pain so every single second of every day they are in some kind of pain. They can't constantly be on painkillers because that is dangerous, they don't want to become addicted and the painkillers don't work as much as they used to.

The constant pain gets to them some days because it is just annoying, they can't do as much as they want and they cannot do a fraction of the things that people without chronic pain do without a second thought.

Sometimes it makes them depressed and this is where the "vice versa" comes in. Our mental health impacts our physical health because mental health conditions like depression, and even our fight-or-flight response, trigger biological responses like increases in inflammation. This only makes our physical health even worse so it becomes a vicious cycle of physical health making our mental health worse which then triggers biological processes then continue to make our physical health worse and so on.

In her book *I Haven't been Entirely Honest With*

You, comedian and actress Miranda Hart explains this interaction very well for laypeople.

Leading me onto the last part of this reflection.

Considering Working in a New Area of Psychology

Don't worry, I still fully intend to work in mental health and one day become a fully qualified clinical psychologist, but Saturday night, I wondered about becoming a health psychologist. Then I shook the silly thought away because I have no intention in doing that.

Yet in my other books and in my lectures, I have learnt that clinical psychologists do work in physical health settings. These include chronic pain management, cancer services, hospice care and so on.

A quick internet search reveals that clinical psychologists help in physical health settings in the following ways:

- Emotional support and coping mechanisms- clinical psychologists help clients to manage their feelings of anxiety, sadness, fear and/ or frustration that often accompany chronic illnesses.
- Therapy- psychologists provide individual or group therapy to help clients adjust to their condition and maintain a good quality of life.
- Work along other professionals from other disciplines- psychologists can work

alongside nurses, doctors and other healthcare professionals to ensure holistic patient care.

- Behavioural intentions- psychologists often assist in developing strategies to improve treatment adherence, pain management and lifestyle changes.
- Consultation and training- psychologists help to educate medical staff on psychological principles that can improve communication as well as patient care.

Sources

British Psychological Society- Guidance for employing practitioner psychologists in physical healthcare settings (2024)

https://www.berkshirehealthcare.nhs.uk/media/109514195/clinical-health-psychologists-psychological-professions.pdf

https://www.nelft.nhs.uk/services-clinical-health-psychology

My Thoughts Continued

I know that clinical psychologists can help people with physical conditions in other ways than medical professionals and after seeing how down and uninterested my partner was because of their physical health. It made a small part of me just want to help them and help others with a physical health condition using a psychological lens.

Of course, I don't think I would ever want this as a job. When I think of myself as a clinical psychologist, I imagine myself talking to clients in a therapy room with depression, anxiety and so on. I still want to work in a primarily mental health setting because I know how horrific mental health conditions can be, so I want to help others.

Still, I think it would be lovely to work in a medical setting for a little while helping people with chronic conditions with my psychological knowledge. Whether this is helping them with pain management, helping them with their outlook on their condition or helping them to come to terms with a hard, life-changing diagnosis.

It's interesting a single subtle moment and a few hours with a partner can change or influence your psychology journey. As much as I hope my partner will be okay sooner rather than later, I am glad we had that conversation.

And I think and hope that my future clients will too.

Are you surprised our physical health can impact our mental health and vice versa?

PACE YOURSELF AFTER TRAUMA RECOVERY, YOUR STRESS POT, FINDING SOLUTIONS AND FEELING OVERWHELMED

I decided to include this reflection in these pages because it will teach you a lot. Firstly, as an aspiring or qualified psychologist, it is normal for you to feel overwhelmed, stressed, and close to burnout at some point in your psychology journey. To be honest, all of us will be close to burnout multiple times because as much as we like to think we know how to avoid it, we aren't always masters of burnout.

Therefore, in this reflection, you'll learn about the values of the Stress Pot exercise, finding solutions and from a clinical viewpoint, you'll get an insight into trauma survivors. Most specifically, a unique challenge that trauma survivors face after healing and recovery.

There are a lot of interesting tips and facts in this reflection, so please enjoy.

***

Silly me for forgetting how important writing is to my mental health.

I'm already starting to feel more relaxed as I sit at my desk with my earphones in listening to the English Cover of the Season 3 theme song of my favourite anime, Demonslayer. There's a wonderfully cool breeze coming from my slightly cracked open window and the keyboard feels good under my fingers as I type away.

There's even the slight taste of orange in my mouth from the massive mug of orange squash that I've made myself.

Whilst this next chapter isn't really explicitly focused on dating after rape, it connects to the wider point of this book. This book is meant to be talking and helping you (and myself) with life after rape and life after you've done the majority of your healing and the worst of your mental health has subsided.

I said "the majority of your mental health symptoms" because there will always be chances of a "flare up". A time when you are triggered, nervous, depressed or you're having a bad day. That's normal for everyone, let alone trauma survivors.

In this book, I've explained how the first time I kissed and made out with my partner, I had massive trauma reactions. Yet I am no longer depressed, I am no longer having severe Post-Traumatic Stress symptoms and I can do so much with my life now that I couldn't do before. That's why I consider myself post-healing and definitely post-rape.

Whether you've reached that point yet doesn't matter. If you keep processing your trauma, working with mental health professionals and take it one day at a time then you will get there in the end. It will always take far longer than you want, but it is possible and you will get there.

Anyway, the reason why I'm writing this chapter is because originally 2025 was meant to be my "comeback" year. After being raped in 2024 and losing the vast majority of the year to my really bad mental health where I was constantly depressed, suicidal and I couldn't function. I wanted 2025 to be the year I went back to pre-rape levels of productivity.

I wanted to do lots of writing, lots of Outreach and university work as well as lots of business work too. Since my writing and author business took a massive hit in 2024 (it fared so much better than I feared) but it still took a hit because I couldn't do much to maintain it. I managed to do the bare minimum.

Therefore, I had a lot of plans and I kept adding things to my To Do List because they would help me fulfil my goals, and in the long term, there could be big rewards. Not only in terms of creativity but these massive projects could save me a lot of time too.

For instance, every single day on YouTube I release a Short, these are 60-second or less audio clips about a psychology fact. I always schedule these about a month in advance or I do a week at a time if I am really pressed for time. Yet doing 30 or 31 YouTube shorts every single month can be a bit of a chore. Hence, why I wanted to do 113 YouTube shorts to schedule it for the next 3 and a bit months in advance so I wouldn't have to touch it again.

Honestly, that would be okay if I didn't have a university exam, my dissertation, my psychology and fiction writing projects and two other massive projects that I'm not going to try and explain in these pages.

Basically, I gave myself a lot to do and for about two months this was okay. I could manage my time and energy levels well enough that I was happy and able to do this much stuff.

However, recently other life stressors have started to pop in and whilst I'll talk about your Stress Pot in a moment. This led me to feel very overwhelmed, very out of control and really burnt out. Honestly, I thought yesterday that I was close to burning out, but in reality, I had already reached burnout.

This meant that I didn't sleep last night because I was so overwhelmed, anxious and I was thinking a lot about how 2025 was the year I was meant to go back to pre-rape levels of productivity.

On a positive note, I didn't have any negative self-talk during last night. I was very self-compassionate and I realised that it was very ambitious in the first place and I needed to seriously cut back on my projects. This meant I didn't feel bad about my situation and my mental health didn't flare up and I didn't get depressed.

This meant I was able to bounce back quicker even though today, I am taking things a lot more slowly.

Lesson For You

As a result, when you finally feel like you've got your life back after your rape, where you can function, you can go outside, you can do whatever you want without having to worry about trauma responses, depression and how impossible it feels to get out of bed in the morning. Firstly, I want to give you a massive congratulations, it's amazing that you've reached this point in your recovery and it shows how far you've come.

Secondly, I want to mention that please pace yourself. You might want to do a million different things and maybe this comes from feeling that you missed out on all the months, years or perhaps decades of your life because of your rape. Yet I would unofficially advise you to go slow for the first year so you, still do as much as you think you can handle. I have flat out loved working on all my fiction and psychology book projects, I have loved doing my YouTube shorts, outreach work and all the other things I do.

It's brought me so much joy, happiness and it makes me grateful to have made as much progress as

I have.

You can do whatever you want too.

Just please be mindful and check in with yourself from time to time. See how you're feeling and make sure that you have "rest time" too so you can relax, unwind and you aren't always going at a million miles per hour.

Just something to bear in mind because it might be frustrating in the short term to have to go slower, but in the long term you'll be grateful and able to do so much more.

Your Stress Pot and Finding Solutions

As soon as I realised I was burnt out, I knew I really needed to think about why I was burnt out. Otherwise, I wouldn't be able to find solutions, fix things and this period of burnout would last a lot longer. I already sort of knew that the main reasons why I was burnt out was because of the massive projects, the sheer amount of things on my To Do List and the lack of time I have this week. Since I'm out basically all weekend.

This is only a five-day week for me and yesterday I spent four hours with my family. Which was lovely, but it was a massive chunk out of my day.

Yet I still felt like there was more to why I was burnt out.

If you're feeling like this, I highly recommend that you do what I did. Get a sheet of A4 paper and draw a pot in the middle and label it *Stress Pot.* I got the idea from *I Haven't Been Entirely Honest With You* by Miranda Hart because she talks about all the little things and her maladaptive ways of living that added to her stress pot until it was too much and her physical and mental health just died.

Afterwards, write down all the different factors that are adding stress into your life. I still maintain because of a brilliant TED Talk and some research studies that stress is not a bad thing. Stress is your body trying to help you deal with a situation and research shows that only people who perceive stress negatively experience negative health outcomes of stress.

My stressors included:

- No one helping me around the house with chores so the house always looks like a mess.
- Not having a lot of time this week.
- Having 3 massive projects on the go.
- Lack of writing time.
- Massive To Do List.
- Stressed about money.
- University work- not knowing how much I've got to do.
- One of my housemates.

There was one more but that's tiny and most of these are simply things that I need to adjust. For example, I rewrote my To Do List and I got rid of a bunch of items until it was basically down to the core essentials of things that I really need to get done this week. This also has extra benefits too, like it gives me more time to write, I've finished one of the massive projects yesterday, did a chunk on another one and the third project I'm not touching this week.

I don't have to deal with the three massive projects anymore this week and it's only Tuesday. That frees me up a lot.

In addition, when it comes to university stuff, I do not recommend this but I was still awake at 00:50 am last night and I wasn't tired. I went on my laptop and looked at my dissertation to see how much it needed to be improved because it was a first draft from over a year ago.

Thankfully, it was in a much better state than I had originally thought and it won't be too much work to improve the first draft. Then this would allow me to send the first draft to my supervisor and now I have a much clearer game plan about what I need to do for my university work. The added bonus of this is that I feel more in control, less overwhelmed and everything is more manageable now.

Essentially, the greatest advantage of doing this Stress Pot exercise is that because all your little and big stressors are right in front of you. You can focus on each one and think about a solution.

There will be some stressors that you will be able to come up with solutions for. Like, what I did with my university work, rewriting my To Do List, letting go of the three massive projects for this week and so on.

On the other hand, there will be stressors that

you cannot do anything about because they are outside of your control. For example, the reason why I am stressed about money is not only because I am near the end of my university journey and I need to find a job because I have rent and bills to pay next year. Yet the far-right is increasing in popularity in the United Kingdom and there is an awful chance that the far-right will become the next government in three years' time. As a gay person that scares me so having enough money to live and weather the awful decisions and hardships that they're going to inflict on the country would be nice.

This is not something I can control and this is something I like to forget about from time to time. Equally, it isn't a big stressor.

What is a big stressor is one of my housemates who has chronic OCD and they are so anxious about exams that they cannot function, they cannot do anything for themselves and even if something is done wrong. They have a massive meltdown. They're like a five-year-old child.

And the thing that bugs me about it is that my housemate can function perfectly fine without a meltdown, a breakdown or crying their eyes out several times a day when their partner (another housemate) isn't about. Whenever their partner is about they turn into a five-year-old child who cannot function without their partner.

It's toxic as anything but the couple admits that everything is fine.

I've tried talking to them about it but this is outside my control, but it affects me because I don't like seeing my best friend (who is the partner) being so burnt out, exhausted and stressed because they have to look after their partner 24/7. So much so they don't have a life outside of the relationship.

And me being attacked for helping the housemate out whenever something isn't clean to OCD-levels, and listening to them cry and scream every day for the past month. That is not fun.

Anyway, living in this environment is not always fun and it is a massive stressor when I have everything else weighing on me too.

A final little tip with this Stress Pot exercise is to number and rank how big the Stressor is in your life. This helps you realise how urgently you might need to try and find a solution. My rankings were:

1. Housemate
2. No one helping me do the chores round the house
3. Massive To Do List
4. Having 3 massive projects on the go
5. Not having a lot of time this week

And so on.

My solution for the housemate and chore situation so the house doesn't look like a shitpit anymore is just to try and talk to them yet again. Even though I know it will not get us anywhere.

Conclusion

On the whole at the end of this chapter, you've

learnt and seen that it's important after rape and trauma healing and recovery to be mindful. As much as we would all love our lives to go back to whatever they were like pre-rape, that isn't the way it works. I don't think this is always a bad thing because there was a lot of post-traumatic growth for me after my rape. I finally fixed my relationship with my family so it's healthier and more enjoyable now.

However. I am still learning and still getting back up to pre-rape speed of productivity and that's okay. Maybe I won't ever get back to those levels of productivity and because I have friends now, a social life and a beautiful partner. Maybe that's a good thing.

Here are some questions to get you thinking at the end of this chapter:

- If you've reached the point in your rape recovery where you can do most things without your mental health impacting you too much, list out everything you do.
- Ask yourself, is this too much? Am I at risk of becoming overwhelmed?
- How could you reduce your feelings of overwhelm and burnout?
- Do the Stress Pot exercise and rank your stressors.
- What solutions could you come up with to reduce the impact of your stressors?

USING AI AVATARS IN CLINICAL PSYCHOLOGY TRAINING

I mean this as a joke but one of the issues with being very popular amongst the lecturers at my university is that I can be walking round the psychology building whilst working as a Student Ambassador, then I can run into a lecturer and suddenly be recruited for a fun psychology study.

Normally, Masters students never have to partake in research studies but this one sounded fun, the Masters students needed clinical people for their sample and I am always happy to help others.

In *Clinical Psychology Reflections Volume 7*, I wrote about my experience with the first part of this study looking at how an artificial intelligence chatbot was pretending to be a client with depression and anxiety. Then I had to interact with the chatbot in a mock psychological assessment situation. In that reflection,

I wrote about the strengths and weaknesses of the chatbot and whether I believed it should be used or not in future clinical psychology training.

Today I had the second part of the study that used a similar structure in terms of I had to conduct a mock psychological assessment with a man with depression and anxiety. Yet this time, the artificial intelligence was a scarily realistic avatar that looked exactly like a real person.

For me, it is just scary how realistic AI is these days and how you can create a real-looking person that I wouldn't be able to tell was artificial intelligence with the press of only a few buttons.

For the next ten minutes, I needed to follow the CBT cross-sectional formulation design to help me gather information for my psychological assessment. I asked him about his home situation, his thoughts, feelings, bodily sensations and suicide, alcohol and substance abuse risk. As well as whether there were any situations that triggered his low mood or anxiety the most.

Another piece of context for the client is that he was an architecture student from an unknown country, and part of his mental health difficulties is that he is struggling to adapt to student life in the UK because he feels lonely.

One of the first issues with the AI avatar is that when I asked him about his home culture he couldn't answer. He only told me about "back home" and "when I moved here". I asked in different ways because I understand in the real world, a client might feel ashamed or concerned about revealing their home country.

The AI avatar still didn't answer so I feel like this was a critical part of background information that I was missing. As well as depending on where the client was from, their home culture probably would have impacted my questions and my ideas for future psychological treatment.

After the ten minutes were up, the researcher came back into the room and she asked me a bunch of open-ended questions about the ethics, advantages and disadvantages of the AI avatar, how I thought it could be improved and so on.

What Are The Positives Of The AI Avatar?

It turns out there are advantages to having an AI Avatar help you in clinical training. I found it helpful that the AI Avatar looked scarily realistic and his responses were very similar and genuinely how I believe a person with depression would respond to my questions. I've given very similar answers in the past, especially during my counselling assessment for my specialist rape counselling when I was experiencing mild depression.

That turned into severe depression a month later.

Therefore, it's useful to have a realistic AI Avatar for trainee clinical psychologists because it allows them to practise clinical skills in a situation similar to the real world. A situation where they would need to carefully word questions, react to what the client was saying and monitor body language.

I'll talk more about body language in the disadvantages section.

In addition, having an AI Avatar could be very useful in clinical training because it means you have to think on your feet. Since the AI Avatar is right there in front of you, you need to think about your responses, practise your active listening skills by showing that you understand what they said and you need to follow up on from their response.

Yet unlike the AI chatbot, you actually need to do this quickly like you would in the real world otherwise you get into awkward silences. Even though in the real world, silence isn't always a bad thing.

On the whole, an AI Avatar might be useful for helping clinical trainees to develop these interpersonal and response skills.

Building upon this advantage, a benefit of the AI Avatar over the chatbot is because I was typing with the chatbot, after a while, I wasn't thoughtful about what I asked and I just asked it. I didn't care about my wording or my phrasing because typing just isn't realistic, it's boring and it was taking a long time to type a response to what the client had just said and my next question.

Nonetheless, when it came to the AI Avatar, I was finding myself being a lot more thoughtful about what I asked because the "client" was right in front of me, blinking and smiling at me.

I had to act as if this was a very real client and I was speaking so it was easier to practise those active listening skills and phrasing my questions in a kind and compassionate way.

Granted, I will be the first to admit that I need to improve this skill. I am not great at knowing how to phrase my questions in certain ways.

Leading me onto my last point, by using the AI Avatar, I was able to identify some areas for improvement. For example, I need to practise wording my questions and responses in a careful and considered manner so I don't offend future clients and risk damaging the therapeutic alliance.

On the whole, I think there are several advantages of an AI Avatar being used in clinical training. For example, AI Avatars can be useful because they look and give realistic responses that can help trainee psychologists get in more practise outside of their placements. This will allow them to improve their clinical skills even more.

In addition, AI Avatars can help trainee psychologists to identify areas for improvement, think more carefully about their responses amongst other benefits.

What Are The Negatives of The AI Avatar?

I've already mentioned how I didn't like that the "client" didn't know where they were from and some of the background information was missing. Yet there were other issues too. For example, I felt that a major issue of the AI avatar was that he looked real, his words were similar to those of a depressed person, but his body language was completely wrong for a depressed or anxious person.

Of course, you could argue that the client with depression was feeling good that day, that he was putting on a brave face and he was trying to trick me as a clinical psychologist that he was doing better than he was. This is possible in the real-world, especially if a client doesn't want to be there and doesn't want psychological support.

This AI Avatar wasn't doing that.

If he was trying to fake his reactions then I ask you the following questions:

- Why was he giving me responses about his presenting problems and other factors that reflect depression in the real-world?
- Why was he encouraging us to solve certain difficulties in therapy sessions?
- Why didn't he mention he was here at someone else's request?

Therefore, I really didn't like how the AI avatar didn't act or show body language similar to that of someone with depression. They didn't look sad, they didn't look nervous and they didn't show that every movement or action was taking a lot of effort.

If the AI avatar had severe depression like it was trying to convince me then he would have showed these behaviours.

Moreover, this is important to note because in a

real-life psychological assessment, a psychologist would be reading and making notes of the client's body language. At the moment, I'm doing an essay assignment where I need to create a psychological treatment programme based on a letter with the results of this client's psychological assessment. The very first section of this letter is about the client's body language during the assessment.

If the AI Avatar does not use body language, how am I meant to improve my ability to read and understand client body language?

I can't.

In addition, when I compare the AI Avatar to the AI chatbot I mentioned in the first part of the study, at least the chatbot mentioned what the client was doing when I asked questions. The chatbot mentioned how the client was picking at a loose piece of their hoodie sleeve, they were biting their lower lip and they were showing other signs of body language.

Surely it is easier for an AI Avatar to show body language, so why didn't it? (besides it not being programmed too).

Another minor issue along the same lines is the tone of voice was slightly wrong, and the small smile the AI Avatar always had was very off-putting. It seemed wrong that the AI Avatar was always smiling even when he was telling me about his depression, how low he felt and how he had considered suicide a few times.

It wasn't realistic in that regard and it was really,

really off-putting.

Therefore, I would highly recommend that if AI Avatars are going to be used in future clinical psychology training then they need to, at the very least, sound like they have depression, sound like they have low mood and they need to not smile as much.

When I was severely depressed in the latter half of 2024, I was not smiling too much, you could hear the depression in my voice and I was not always even remotely happy.

These AI Avatars are, and it just doesn't match up with what the AI Avatar is saying.

Finally, besides from being a little repetitive because sometimes regardless of the question I asked, he gave me very similar answers to previous questions so I wasn't always able to get the information I needed for my psychology assessment. One issue I didn't have with the AI Avatar was that he was meant to be experiencing depression and anxiety, he got the depression, he didn't get the anxiety.

He didn't tell me about having sweaty hands, feeling panicked and overwhelmed and he didn't tell me about any situations that he felt anxious in.

As a result, this leads me to one of the disadvantages I mentioned to the researcher, I do not think that AI Avatars will be useful in training clinical psychologists to support those with more "complex" mental health conditions. For example, psychosis, those with personality disorders, trauma responses and those with hallucinations and delusions.

If an AI Avatar that is meant to show depression and anxiety can only show one condition that we know a lot about, then I am concerned how an AI Avatar will manage to accurately represent a more complex condition. Since if we take obsessive-compulsive disorder for example, it is not only handwashing and being clean. OCD can encompass a lot more.

Here is a small extract from an episode of The Psychology World Podcast focusing on OCD:

"DSM-5 includes other information in the diagnostic criteria. For example, the obsessions or compulsions take up more than one hour a day, cause impairment for the person and/ or they cause clinically significant levels of distress. Then there is the typical DSM-5 caveat that Obsessive Compulsive Disorder needs to be the best explanation for what the client is experiencing and their symptoms cannot be better explained by another mental health or medical condition or a substance.

When it comes to the obsessions themselves, the specific details of them can vary wildly between different people with Obsessive Compulsive Disorder. They can include thoughts round contamination, a desire for order or they can be taboo thoughts around harm to themselves or others, sex and/ or religion."

As you can see, there is a lot of variation in OCD so I think it would be very difficult to accurately programme an AI Avatar to show this range of behaviours. Then I think it is "dangerous" or "unhelpful" to our future clients if we train trainee psychologists with an Avatar that reinforces and only shows stereotypes.

Just a thought.

Would I Recommend The AI Avatar For Clinical Training?

Personally, with the rise of artificial intelligence and how it is impacting more aspects of our lives. I strongly believe that at some point artificial intelligence will be a part of clinical psychology whether we like it or not. I already talked about artificial intelligence and chatbots to some extent in clinical psychology because of mental health apps in my book *Could Apps Improve Our Mental Health*?

However, when it comes to whether I would recommend AI Avatars in clinical training. I would say not at this current moment in time but in the future, I think there is definitely a place for AI Avatars.

I can see AI Avatars being very useful in the beginning of clinical training because it will help trainees develop and extra practise in those core competencies that they will be using every single day with clients. They'll be able to practise their active listening, communication and relationship-building skills with the AI Avatars.

Also, AI Avatars will be useful because instead of trainees only being able to practise these skills with real-world clients during business hours. Trainees will be able to practise whenever they want.

However, these AI Avatars are not perfect and they have limited uses at the moment. Before I highly recommend these avatars for clinical training, they need to be more realistic in the terms of body language and voice tone so trainees can develop their body language monitoring skills too.

In addition, the AI Avatars need more background information, especially if they are meant to be someone who has recently moved to the region or country because their culture of origin could be critical to understanding the social factors underpinning their mental health condition.

Then there are other disadvantages too that I mentioned earlier in the chapter.

I think there is a place for AI Avatars and there is great potential for this technology in training so our trainees can become even better at helping our amazing clients. I just don't think we're there yet.

What do you think?

YOU DON'T HAVE TO BE PERFECT, YOU'RE HUMAN AFTER ALL

This next reflection, I believe, will be controversial but please bear with me and I am always happy to hear about both sides of the source of this reflection whether you agree or disagree with me.

Before I dive into the heart of this topic, I wanted to caveat everything by saying that as aspiring and qualified psychologists, we need to try to be perfect, or at least try to get as close as possible to "perfect" as we can. We need to be the best therapists and mental health practitioners that we can be.

We need to actively listen to clients without judgment, and we need to listen with empathy, compassion and understanding.

Of course, we will make mistakes and we will not be perfect with every client. That is okay. As long as we reflect and learn from our mistakes then that is all anyone can ask of us and we will learn, get better and do better in the future. So the mistakes don't repeat themselves and we can be better with the next client.

You Don't Have To Be Perfect Outside the Therapy Room

However, I don't believe that we need to be an idealised psychologist-self in our personal life to some extent because this will only lead to burnout, we will deny ourselves emotional rest and this will only harm our ability to help our clients in our job.

In this reflection, I am talking about what if one of your friends or housemates or loved ones has a mental health condition that is stressing you out, draining you and you are having to deal with it every hour of every day. It will be different if they are a family member, your child or your partner.

For the purposes of this reflection, I am not really talking about those situations but some of the lessons still apply here.

Instead, for the purposes of this reflection, I am talking about what if a housemate or friend of yours has a mental health condition that is really taxing you. I'll use a personal example that inspired this reflection.

I live in a house with my friends who are all university students, and one of the people I live with has Obsessive-Compulsive Disorder so things need to be done a certain way. Also, they have depression, anxiety and trauma. That means they are often too depressed to move and coupled with their chronic health and chronic pain, this makes life very difficult for them.

However, what annoys me is that my OCD housemate can cook for themselves, function and make themselves a drink when their partner (another housemate) isn't at the house for a few days. They can function okay without having breakdowns, crying and screaming every day like clockwork.

Yet as soon as their partner is home, they have breakdowns every day, they cannot cook or eat for themselves and etc.

In addition, because of their OCD, they micromanage everything because everything has to be done a certain way. For instance, at the moment, we have a flying ant infestation in the house and on the second day, I was too grossed out by it so I went to get some ant killer. I said ant repellent in my messages because I didn't know there was a difference.

I'm new to this, okay.

Anyway, my OCD housemate kept asking me if I had read the label, if I knew how to do it and every single little thing I did wasn't enough. They kept asking their partner to do it better (because they wouldn't do it themselves) so I simply had enough, I didn't want to deal with the ants anymore because I knew I wouldn't do it good enough.

Anyway, you could argue that because my OCD housemate has OCD, they have depression, they have anxiety and they have chronic health conditions that I should be perfectly accommodating. I should treat them like a client and always listen and deal with them in a compassionate, empathetic and non-judgemental way.

I would say you have a point but you don't live in this situation 24 hours a day 7 days a week. You don't see how my best friend burns themselves out looking after my OCD housemate even though my OCD housemate can function and do things for themselves.

In addition, I used to be really patient, I used to listen and help a lot. Yet because their partner keeps accommodating and reinforcing their OCD habits, the OCD is only getting worse and I am so fed up with nothing I do being good enough because of their OCD. And my OCD housemate isn't even trying to deal with their OCD and that is what really bugs me.

Honestly, my mental health is a lot better since I stopped wanting to look after them or even help them. I know a lot of readers might think that is harsh and very bad as an aspiring clinical psychologist. Yet if you are one of those readers, I think you forget that it is normal for clinical psychologists to become annoyed and irritated with the clients that they get to see in their job.

For example, sometimes you know as a clinical psychologist what the client needs to do to improve their lives, but they aren't willing to see it or do it.

As long as we are never rude to our clients, we reflect on why it annoyed us and we try to be better in the future with our clients then that's okay.

Yet when it is a friend or housemate, it is

draining living with someone with OCD and another mental health condition. You are always stressed, you are always concerned about doing or moving anything because you don't want to cause the person with OCD to have a meltdown and you don't want to cause your OCD friend any more distress than they already are.

It is so emotionally and mentally draining that I was done supporting my housemate a long time ago, and I am happy for doing it.

I feel happier in myself, my mental health is better and I am not as burnt out as I used to be because I am no longer allowing my housemate's OCD to consume my energy.

This is self-care for me.

Therefore, I want to stress at the end of this reflection that just because you are an aspiring or qualified clinical psychologist, it doesn't mean you have to be a perfect clinical psychologist 100% of the time every second of every day. You are a human being.

You are allowed to be angry, annoyed and irritated by your friends or family members with mental health conditions. As long as you provide kindness, support and love when needed and as long as you look after yourself then sometimes, that is all you need to do.

Or all you can do as harsh as it might sound to some people. Especially, if your friend or loved one has no drive or motivation to change their maladaptive coping mechanisms.

You can't force people to take steps towards improving their mental health. Only they can do that when it is the right time for them.

And sadly, sometimes that does mean just living with the consequences.

Look after yourself dear reader. You're important and you don't have to be perfect. You are a wonderful, kind and caring human after all.

But we all have our limits.

EMOTIONAL FATIGUE

No matter what anyone tells you, you don't have to be an empathy machine 24/7 that always pumps out empathy, understanding and all the other amazing qualities we give our clients 24 hours a day seven days a week.

You are allowed to be human.

You are allowed to be angry. You are allowed to be annoyed. You are allowed to give up on people and understand that there is nothing *you* can do to help them and it is better for your mental health to walk away and distance yourself.

Dear reader, I am emotionally fatigued and exhausted.

I simply don't want to do this anymore.

I would honestly forgive you if you think I'm a fully qualified mental health professional who actively sees clients because that is a common statement in mental health professions. Yet no, I am simply emotionally exhausted because of my toxic living situation and it has all come to a head recently, as well as other people have helped me realise that it truly isn't me being blinded and I am not at fault.

I am still a human being so I will never be perfect but I am not at fault here, everyone else agrees with me and I am not a horrible person.

Anyway, the situation will become clear in a moment.

However, first of all, I wanted to put this in a clinical psychology context in a few different ways. Firstly, emotional fatigue and emotional burnout in mental health professions, including clinical psychology, are extremely high and problematic. Clinical psychologists see clients every single day for an hour at a time, we hear their most distressing experiences, we have to support them and help them and we have to deal with management, understaffing, underfunding, our personal lives and so many other factors.

I always say that clinical psychologists are trusted with a client's deepest, darkest secrets, experiences and thoughts. That is brilliant in therapy because it means our clients trust us and we can get more information and we can help them.

Yet it comes with a price too if mental health professionals don't practise self-care, strike a good work/ life balance and so on. It leads to emotional burnout.

And despite what a lot of laypeople believe,

empathy is a finite resource. We don't have endless amounts of empathy and we can't be dealing with high, intense emotions and psychologically distressed people 24/ 7 without it negatively impacting us.

This is why burnout in mental health professionals and healthcare in general is so high.

In addition, I've spoken to clinical psychologists at my university and they experience a good few clients who don't have a capacity for change. It frustrates them, it bugs them and it hurts them a little because if you have a client who doesn't want to put in the work to undergo therapeutic change. As well as if you've worked with them as much as you can to understand why they don't have a motivation to change and there's nothing you can do. Then it's disappointing because you want to help this person, it's why we all want to get into this job but this client doesn't want to do the work. So they use up a session that could be used by someone else.

Someone who wants to change.

My entire point is that being around all these high, intense emotions all day at work is tiring. Hell, any physically, emotionally, mentally demanding job is demanding and taxing on us. Therefore, some of the clinical psychologists, I've spoken to absolutely love just going home and being a mum, a dad, a friend, a partner and anyone but a psychologist.

And when you take off that psychologist hat, you don't have to be the perfectly understanding, empathetic and compassionate person without fault.

Of course, everyone who wants to become a clinical psychologist or mental health professional, like myself, shares certain qualities.

We are lovely, determined, resilient, understanding and we are kind, friendly and supportive people in general.

Yet we are still human too and part of this is setting healthy boundaries in place so we can look after ourselves and not be exhausted. Looking after ourselves today means we can be there for our clients tomorrow and the next day and the day after that.

A few evenings ago, my friend texted me and asked me to go to the hospital with him and unfortunately a friend of his tried to kill himself. I was physically free to take him but I was socially and mentally exhausted, and I was a little physically exhausted too. So I could have taken him, thankfully he has another friend with a car so I wasn't too worried, but there would have been a price for me to pay.

A high one.

I would have been even more exhausted and my mental health would have suffered a lot.

I couldn't support my friend by physically taking him somewhere, but I compromised. I texted him later saying that I was always there for him to talk and we had a little conversation about how *he* was doing. And I will honestly ask him to meet up in the next few weeks because I want to check on him.

Sometimes as unpopular or against popular

culture saying no and setting a boundary that focuses on us might be, it is what is needed.

This is something that my rape counselling taught me. Myself, my needs and my mental health will always be the most important thing even if other people get annoyed by it.

I mention this because for me, at the moment, I am working a lot of Outreach work at my university. This means I am working 8-hour days running sessions, presenting content and interacting with a lot of students and young people. I've been working with hundreds of 13-year-olds at the moment on different events.

I am autistic, I am introverted and I have a stutter at times. Presenting and leading sessions is like performing to me. I flat out love it and I would love to never ever give it up, but it takes energy. Interacting with so many young people, teachers and other ambassadors takes energy too.

When I come home, ideally, this is a stress-free, fun and relaxing environment that recharges me because I'm living with my friends, I'm able to do my own projects and I'm able to decompress.

At the moment I am not able to do that at all, so I am always using up emotional energy and this has burnt me out.

Living at home burns me out. That is sad and tragic.

On the whole, this reflection wasn't meant to be as long as it's turned out to be, so I'll explain the toxic living situation and why I've reached emotional fatigue in the next reflection.

However, in terms of practical lessons for you as an aspiring or qualified clinical psychologist, here's what I would say:

- Remember you and your mental health are the most important thing.
- It is okay to say no to people.
- Practise self-care to prevent burnout as much as possible.
- Understand emotional fatigue and the signs.
- Understand you don't need to be an empathy machine 24/ 7.
- It's good to be more than a psychologist.

Back in Clinical Psychology Reflections Volume 6, I reflected on why the best psychologists are well-rounded people.

Check it out and now let's move on to the fun chaos that sparked this reflection.

TOXIC LIVING SITUATIONS AND YOU DON'T HAVE TO BE AN EMPATHY MACHINE TO BE A PSYCHOLOGIST

In the last reflection, I discussed emotional fatigue in clinical psychology and if you haven't already, I highly, highly recommend that you read or listen to that reflection because it puts this reflection into perspective.

In this next reflection, I want to explain the impact of toxic living situations, why because you are a human being with faults and all, you won't be an empathy machine all the time and that's a good thing. And it is okay if you don't get on with every single person with a mental health condition.

And I'll discuss a lot more facets too as well as how this applies to clinical psychologists and ourselves.

At the end of this reflection, I do explain how

this can apply to you and other aspiring and qualified psychologists.

Finally before we dive into what happened, I want to mention that you might read this reflection and think I made mistakes, you would have done things differently and you might have handled everything better or worse compared to me. Everyone is honestly validate in their thoughts on this because you are different to me. You have your own attitudes, backgrounds and experiences so maybe you would handle something better than me.

Maybe I would handle someone better than you because I have strengths you might not, but my weaknesses might be your strengths.

All of us can only do our best in the moment, learn from our mistakes if we make any and we can just keep going forward.

One step at a time.

What Happened?

I've written in a few places about my non-ideal living situation. I live in shared university housing with a friend of mine and a couple. We all used to be friends but the couple has really made that difficult, because to cut a long story short, the couple we live with have a very clingy, toxic relationship.

Originally at first me and the friend I live with (Let's call her Lauren) thought we were wrong about this and it was only us who thought this. It took us a lot of time to actually admit our own annoyances and concerns over the relationship to each other. Then we ended up bonding over it and actually coming good friends that way.

Oliver (a fake name) has a very unfortunate habit of getting into relationships with people who need a lot of mental health and physical support, and that is not a problem in its own right. Yet in Oliver's relationships, he always becomes a carer and he always ends up being a full-time carer instead of a partner. Oliver gives up their friends, their own interests and their entire life becomes about supporting and loving their partner, in this case Jane.

As well as Jane has Obsessive-Compulsive Disorder, depression, anxiety and she is recovering from childhood trauma. And I will talk more about how I've tried to support her as much as I humanly can in a moment, but she is so dependent on Oliver that she cannot function at all without him.

Oliver and Jane are each other's entire lives.

Again, part of me believed this was me being unfair and biased, because maybe I was just being emotionally fatigued. Since I am always around Jane's breakdowns, screaming, crying and being so overwhelmed by the smallest things.

However, today, I was at a friend's house playing board games and it was a brilliant day. I got talking to two friends at the house and they completely agreed, they actually brought it up about Oliver's relationships.

Oliver and Jane went round this friend's house to watch Eurovision a few weeks ago and I didn't go because there wasn't enough room. And I was enjoying spending time with my ex-partner at the time anyway.

And one of these friends mentioned to me today that Jane is a literal child. She is so clingy, she is so needy and Jane made her so uncomfortable because she was acting like a child towards Oliver.

We were saying how we understand this can sometimes be a kink thing that people do behind closed doors, similar to dom and sub stuff. Yet when it is 24/ 7 and the relationship becomes a caring role instead of a loving relationship then this is not healthy.

For another piece of context, me and this particular friend both have rape and trauma experience similar to Jane so we understand what it's like. And this friend mentioned how this is a pattern with Oliver, this is what he always does and it never ends well.

Especially because Jane is so dependent on Oliver, what happens if they break up? How will Jane function?

Back to me, dear reader.

Jane was a friend a while ago and as a friend, I tried, I honestly tried to do a lot for her, because I've been where she is right now. Just read any of my rape-related books to see how I was having panic attacks at everything, I couldn't leave the house without having a mental breakdown and I tried to kill myself three times in 2024.

I couldn't get out of bed, I was so depressed all the time and so on.

This is why I asked how Jane was, I took her to places, I watched her Minecraft streamers with her when I really don't like Minecraft. I listened to her talk for hours about her autistic special interests even though she never wanted to hear about mine and a lot of other stuff.

Yet recently, it's just been getting to the point where I cannot do this anymore. I am so stressed about living here and being scared about Jane's breakdowns and I hate hearing her cry and scream and her mental health symptoms attacking me that it has left me burnt out.

I was really burnt out the other week when we had a flying ant infestation at the house and I was not impressed. The ants were disgusting and I will admit and I am not afraid to mock myself here. I confirmed every gay stereotype with my handling of the flying ants.

It was gross.

Yet on the second day of the flying ant nightmare, I purchased some ant killer powder and Jane micromanaged me because of her OCD. She asked me a hundred different questions and nothing I did to handle the flying ant situation was good enough for her. I left the situation because I was angry that she didn't trust me to deal with a simple situation on my own.

I got Oliver to deal with it instead.

Then yesterday we went to Aldi, a cheap German retailer here in the UK, and this week I have been working 8-hour days like I mentioned in the last reflection. I flat out love Outreach work, I love working with my fellow ambassadors and working in education is so rewarding and fun. Yet to work 8-hours, come home to have to do all the housework and dishwasher because Jane cannot do things because of her mental health, and Oliver is so focused on looking after Jane, he cannot help.

As well as I have my dissertation to do improvements on and a bunch of my own projects to do.

I was so close to being physically exhausted.

Yet Jane wanted to go to Aldi on Tuesday because they wanted food and I don't want them to starve. I came to a compromise with myself that I take her Friday morning because if I took her before then, I would 100% be burnt out. Friday morning minimised that risk.

Yet Jane didn't thank me to taking her and when I tried to be friendly by sharing a happy moment with her, she shut me down.

And she had a bunch more breakdowns when we got home and I had to listen to all of it because the walls and ceiling in the house are so thin. It was draining me and I wasn't happy about the Aldi situation because I wanted to be thanked considering I really didn't have to do it.

Personally, I feel like living here is not relaxing, it

does not recharge me and I am always stressed. I am always avoiding Jane and Oliver because it is so awkward between us all because we don't get on and we don't have a relationship. This is largely because Oliver and Jane are so focused on each other, it is impossible to have a conversation with either of them.

That's a whole different story.

So I needed to end the friendship yesterday with Jane and I needed to set a boundary that I couldn't take them anywhere anymore because it was too emotionally draining for me. I always felt bad afterwards and I am spending my energy doing my Outreach work, my projects and other things. I needed to look after myself and my energy levels.

I sent a very kind text and I showed it to Lauren and she said it was fine. It was kind, compassionate and to the point.

Jane and Oliver did not agree so we had a meeting about it.

That is where this reflection came from.

The meeting didn't really go anywhere because Oliver does all the talking for Jane so Oliver thinks I lack all empathy, I have no self-reflection, I am cold and I should not be a clinical psychologist. He believes I blame Jane for their mental "illness" (even though I refuse to call it an illness because that is very medical and judgmental language) and that wasn't my intention with my message to Jane.

The meeting was a disaster and me and Oliver

agreed that something needed to change because we can't do this for another year but I don't have hope. It's so draining living here and I wish I had never signed the tenancy renewal.

I just can't do this anymore.

I know my words cannot express what it is like living here and being around Jane 24-hours a day, 7 days a week for a year and constantly having to try and support someone's mental health in addition to working on your own mental health a few months ago and everything else I do with my life.

Especially, when Jane and Oliver are each other's lives and they don't give me anything in return.

I wanted to set boundaries and protect my wellbeing.

Self-Reflection

Of course, I am not perfect and over the past 6 months, I have moved heaven and earth to become a better person. It was one of the reasons why I researched sexual violence, rape recovery and read a few workbooks so I could heal from my rape and stop impacting and hurting everyone round me because of my trauma.

I was hurting people.

Oliver was my entire support network, I was having panic attacks, screaming and I was having extreme trauma responses to anything. I was hell to live with and I feel so sorry for Oliver, Jane and Lauren for the first few months of living with me.

Thankfully, when Oliver dropped me (we were

only ever friends) and replaced me with Jane, I learnt how to stand on my own two feet.

When I realised I was hurting people with my anorexia. Oliver and Lauren were constantly worried about me, I was scaring them with my lack of eating and my weight loss. I realised protecting my friends was an important reason for going to anorexia counselling, reading my workbook and changing my life for the better.

Finally, for this section, when I finally realised just how badly my disorganised attachment style was ruining my life, and how I was messing up so many friendships because of my abuse. I read books, researched and did workbooks to become more securely attached and I've changed my life for the better.

As well as I've written 8 clinical psychology books entirely focused on reflections and improving myself as an aspiring clinical psychologist as well as I've written four rape-related books focusing on sexual violence, what happened to me and how this could help me in the future.

I am not perfect. I am seriously not but I do learn and I do improve my life. I do self-reflect.

Empathy

If you ever asked me, why do I write my psychology books and why do I do the podcast every single week since 11th November?

If you asked me, why do I do my Outreach work? Why do I present sessions? Why do I overwork myself?

If you asked me, why do I want to be a clinical psychologist?

There is a simple answer, because I want to help people. I want to help through my books and podcast to understand and love psychology as much as I do, and I want to keep learning.

I want to help amazing students and young people that regardless of your background, regardless of your socioeconomic status and regardless of your race that university is a great option for you if you want to go.

I want to help people with mental health difficulties to decrease their psychological distress, improve their lives and develop more adaptive coping mechanisms.

That all requires empathy and I love that. I love interacting with people, I love sharing and understanding their feelings.

I understand what it is like to be so depressed that you cannot get out of bed, I understand what it is like to try and kill yourself because you see no other way out. I understand what it is like to be so terrified of a friend because of your rape.

It turns out that because of one of the ways how my trauma responses manifested nine months ago, Jane is scared of me because of non-me-related trauma reasons. Shortly after my rape, I was terrified of Oliver because of some attraction stuff and Oliver is lovely and would never ever hurt me.

I understand what it is like to have trauma make you irrationally scared of a friend. It is awful and I do not wish it on anyone.

My ex-partner said when they broke up with me that I was lovely, really sweet and so nice because of how caring and empathetic I was towards them despite how "badly" they had treated me by not letting us go on dates because their chronic physical and mental health was so bad.

You can read about all these events in any of my rape-related books for the full story and context.

And in the beginning, I cared about Jane so much, I hated seeing them distressed and I tried to move heaven and earth to make them feel even remotely better.

I got burnt out, my mental health suffered and when my mental health was at its worse after my rape, their distress made me even more distressed.

It has never worked and I cannot deal with it anymore, but to say I shouldn't be a clinical psychologist because I don't have self-reflection and I don't have empathy is a mistake.

I am just burnt out trying to live with and support Jane and do a million other things that my life requires.

I cannot do everything and I cannot support someone without anything back. A friendship is a two-way street and I need to protect myself because I don't want to return to where Jane is.

I am important too.

What Does This Mean for Aspiring and Qualified Psychologists?

I understand that there were things I have written above that were clumsily worded and you really need to be living here and know Oliver and Jane personally to understand the full extent of it. However, I am writing this reflection to help you understand, maybe not now but maybe in the future, that it is good to walk away from people in need if it means you and your mental health will be okay.

I admire the hell out of Oliver for being able to support Jane 24-hours a day, seven days a week, but me, Lauren and everyone else who knows Oliver can see the price. As soon as Oliver and Jane got together, Oliver has stopped talking to friends, they have stopped going out, they have stopped going to Dungeons and Dragons as much.

Their entire life as become about supporting Jane unconditionally.

Jane's and Oliver's comment earlier about I shouldn't be a clinical psychologist because I've run out of empathy for Jane is wrong.

I just have a healthy balance and I know I need to prioritise myself instead of supporting a friend and loved one no matter what.

So do you.

When I went for my rape counselling, in a really distressed and scared state, I asked my rape counsellor if I would be able to become a psychologist if Jane's distress and me worrying about her impacts me so much. She said supporting friends and clients are completely different because you can compartmentalize and you can leave your work at the office.

In other words, she, a mental health professional, was telling me that being a psychologist is about knowing the difference between supporting a client professionally where you show empathy, non-judgmental and compassionate concern and all the other interpersonal skills that a psychologist needs. And being able to go home and decompress and recharge your emotions.

I hadn't realised that until the past few days that was what I was missing in my life.

Therefore, my dear reader, I am human and I am not perfect. I get angry, I get annoyed and I am not empathetic 24/7 and I am not a psychologist 24/7. Some people reading this might think that is a mistake and I am a bad person for doing it.

Yet I am doing the best I can possibly can in a living situation that constantly stresses me and it is awkward and filled with microaggressions. It is why Lauren is still living at home over summer with her family because it is more peaceful there, even though Lauren is still paying rent here for the six months she isn't living here.

Lauren's mental health is way better because she isn't living here.

Therefore, right or wrong, I am not angry or sad or annoyed at myself for setting boundaries that will protect my wellbeing and mental health, even if it means I cannot be as empathetic as I would like to be towards Jane. I just get burnt out too easily.

And if I get burnt out in any way, be it physically, emotionally, mentally or any other type of burnout. Then it means I cannot interact with the amazing students or young people, readers or listeners or any future clients I flat out love helping and supporting.

And neither can you.

FINDING OUT THE WORSE ABOUT SOMEONE IN YOUR SOCIAL NETWORK

Note: for the purposes of this reflection, I want to make it clear, the anomalous subject of this reflection has done absolutely nothing wrong legally, only ethically and morally depending on your beliefs.

Also, potential trigger warnings are possible references to implied paedophilic tendencies.

Our next reflection is definitely something I never normally talk about because normally, something this major, this disgusting and this alarming never pops up in my social networks. Yet when me and some friends discussed it in depth, the implications and what this means for our friendship group, I was rather disturbed for two days. Since this has larger implications for me because I have to spend more time with this person than the rest of our friends.

Due to the topic and nature of this book, I am keeping even more details out for the sake of privacy than normal.

Why Am I Reflecting on This Experience in A Clinical Psychology Book?

Before I explain the situation and what disgusting thing I realised about someone I am somewhat close with, I want to stress the reason why I am talking about it in a clinical psychology reflection book is because there are stark implications for us as aspiring and qualified psychologists.

As well as just people in society, because whenever certain topics come up, like possible sexual abuse, manipulation and pedo-tendencies. It is very common (unfortunately) to brush it under the rug and not do something about it.

As normal people in society, we might want to kick, scream and decry those people that didn't raise concerns about their friend's behaviour sooner. We should and as a society, we should stand up to this behaviour as soon as we see it.

Yet as my example shows, it is very, very difficult.

What Happened?

For a long time, me and my friends have been concerned and joked about another friend's, let's call him Bob, dating behaviour. As a result of me being so disturbed for two days, I sent my best friend a message to explain the situation and I wanted her feedback.

I've stripped out a lot of details for the sake of privacy.

"In the Social group, the standing joke is Bob dates children. Ex 1 was 22 years old when they dated but looked 12, Current Partner at times looks like a 12-year-old boy, Ex Number 2 was 22 looked 12 (even my Mum agrees). I've seen the majority of Bob partners and the joke tracks. Also, the Social Group has massive issues with Bob (25) hooking up with Tokito (18). If we look at Current Partner, they act like a child and cling to Bob. Bob is like a parent.

Everyone is very uncomfortable with this dating pattern of Bob always dating people who are much younger than them, look it and act like children round Bob. My Friend said "if Tokito wasn't so tall, they would look like a child,"

It's a little pedo. Another Friend works for the police and he wants distance from Bob for his job.

There's a minor predatory angle too. Bob (24) told me they met Tokito (18) at Freshers' week after playing board games, saw Tokito and thought "cute, queer person". Bob started talking to Tokito and invites Tokito to *the event this social group was formed around* to spend more time with them.

A few months later, they hooked up with a 6-year age gap.

This is the short version. They're having a serious talk about banning Bob from *the event social group was formed around* because they don't want to be associated with Bob's dating behaviour. And Bob doesn't make a friendship effort with them either. I'm still invited to *the event social group was formed around*.

Putting me in an awkward position. The group wants to say to Bob "sorry *the event social group was formed around* isn't on this year," but how awkward is it if Bob finds out I'm still playing with them?

I'm trying to cut a lot out for you but I'm really uncomfortable with Bob knowing their dating behaviour, how they always make their partners dependent on them, and how they only became friends with Tokito because they're cute and then Bob hooked up with them.

I'm really uncomfortable about that. I know I know a lot more about Bob, their other friends and relationships than you, but if you're comfortable I would really like your thoughts on this."

I hope the general gist of the text message was clear and the whole reason why this popped up in the friendship group was because they were all starting to question was when does the joke about Bob dating children, stop becoming a joke and it becomes a real concern.

In reality, I genuinely wouldn't have been surprised if Bob had dated, slept with or done something with a 16 or 17 year old when they were older than that. Even though that is the age of consent in the UK, I am still concerned.

In addition, Bob's partners rarely have the

physical and mental health to stand up for themselves. They always, always have a range of mental health and physical health needs that mean it is easy for Bob to be a saviour and get his partner to rely on him.

Anyway, this led to a very awkward conversation with my friends because it is a situation all of us need to navigate. Yet there were threads I wanted to pull based on clinical psychology and general society.

No One Wanted To Confront Bob or Challenge Him

The general consensus after all our conversations was that even though everyone wanted to distance themselves from Bob because their pedo-dating behaviour is alarming. No one wanted to tell Bob this was why they were wanting distance.

This is a hard decision for all of us because Bob was a dear friend. He is a lovely person, very kind, very caring and he is a generally good person to be round.

Reflecting more generally, if we think about the public news stories about celebrities who have been found out to be paedophiles. The general public thought they seemed lovely, kind and great people.

Therefore, we don't want to distance or lose a good friend and someone we like. Yet when their dating behaviour of basically dating children has been this consistent of a pattern and it makes everyone really uncomfortable. Then we do need to think about distancing ourselves.

Yet the consensus on how to distance ourselves was to simply say "the event isn't on this year,". They didn't want to have the conversation about Bob's behaviour, that their concerned and they don't approve of Bob.

Mainly, this comes from a fear of massive conflict, massive arguments and they really don't want to hurt Bob.

From a clinical psychology or a more informed point of view as a layperson, I think it's reasonable to assume this is how other people round sexual predators feel. Most of the time, until the survivors come forward, they are only guessing, they are only thinking about their concerns and what they see.

It is very hard to challenge someone, like Bob, without any proof, any evidence or without a survivor coming forward. Therefore, whilst I maintain that the people round the sexual predator are always partly to blame because they could have stepped up, voiced concerns and more.

I understand how difficult, nerve-racking and impossible it feels. And the easiest way is to just not say anything.

Equally, you could argue that I should say something to Bob. If I have the balls and the courage to reflect on this experience in a book, surely I should just say this to Bob's face.

I cannot because if Bob truly, truly hates me then a very important aspect of my life gets even more complex, toxic and awful.

Again for privacy reasons, I won't point-blank explain more.

There Was Denial From My Best Friend

In addition, another implication of this entire situation was when I sent that message to my best friend. They were immediately in denial, they were gently questioning whether I was wrong, maybe we had all misunderstood things and they were trying to come up with excuses for why that wasn't the case.

Traditionally, I would agree with my best friend without a shadow of a doubt because she knows Bob in the same exact way I do. She's friends with Bob and no one wants to think that their friend is capable of something like this.

Yet in my experience, when other people bring up the exact same concerns that you've been hiding for months, and you have never mentioned these fears to these other people. Chances are you are all correct because you have all noticed the exact same patterns independently.

That is concerning.

Nonetheless, as my best friend showed, denial behaviour is powerful. It is the default response and as you'll see in a moment, I was no different at first. In fact, everything involved in these conversations was no different at first.

It was why my friends joked about Bob dating children at first because it was so much easier than realising, there might actually be some truth in the matter.

Denial From Me

In case you've read my book, *Dating After Rape,*

you might know that Tokito is the fake name I gave to my first-ever relationship. Tokito broke up with me after 14-weeks together because their chronic health was so bad, they didn't have time or energy to date.

I know it sounds like an excuse but I swear given everything about Tokito, that isn't a lie.

Anyway, this is why I was in denial for so long about Bob's behaviour because I didn't want to think about Bob and Tokito doing it, and how Bob might have played the long game with Tokito to sleep with them.

Given everything I know about Tokito's life and past experiences, I never want them to go through that.

Ultimately, there were a lot of feelings, emotions and thoughts I needed to process when I finally realised that Bob does date people who look really, really young and they "target" freshers. They basically "target" people who are round the age of 18 and look younger.

That really creeped me out and it took me two days to stop being disturbed by it.

This doesn't mean I am okay with it. I am seriously not. If I was perfectly okay, I wouldn't be writing this reflection a week later, but I am concerned.

And because of how me and Bob are connected through a toxic situation (hint, hint), I don't want to rock the boat too much. Yet if Bob gets kicked out of this social group, I am going to keep going and Bob is going to start to question why he was told it wasn't on.

I don't know if I could keep the truth from him forever about how everyone feels about him, his dating behaviour and his partners.

Conclusion

Ultimately, at the end of this reflection, I want to confirm again that we have no idea if Bob has ever done something illegal, and there might be some readers thinking me and my friends are simply overreacting to massive age gaps and Bob having sex with people who look like 12-year-olds.

However, the reason for this reflection was to perhaps inspire a little bit of empathy towards the people round sexual predators, as long as they didn't help, support or encourage the predatory behaviour.

Chances are they did see the patterns, they did want to speak up and they did want to challenge the possible predator. But without evidence, without wanting to cause a massive conflict and argument and without wanting to damage social networks, it is really hard.

It is even harder when we remember some of the most famous sexual predators on the news are very rich, very powerful and very influential people. Individuals who could ruin a friend if they challenged them.

Just something to think about.

REMEMBER PEOPLE CAN CHANGE

I wrote a similar version of this reflection for my book, *Dating After Rape*, that gives you the other side of this reflection but this is something I've noticed a few different times over the past few months and this is something that I really don't like, it is something that takes time to change and it can lead to a bit of self-doubt in individuals with mental health difficulties. Yet as loved ones, psychology students and professionals, this makes perfect sense.

And this is the perception that people are wary about believing people with mental health conditions about how well they are doing.

I want to say upfront that I understand where this is coming from, because mental health conditions, especially depression, anorexia, trauma amongst others, make a person isolate themselves. This makes them say things like "I'm fine," "you don't understand," "what's the point" when we ask how they are and more.

However, there are times when someone with mental health difficulties is actually okay and they can be okay for the long term.

Let me give you a more practical example from my own life. Then towards the end of the chapter, I'll explain how us aspiring and qualified psychologists can learn from this as professionals and people too.

My Example

My best friend always mentioned from time to time how I'm mentally "ill" (I hate that pathologising language as an aspiring clinical psychologist) and they believe that I am never doing as well as I say I am. Partly, it is like they are waiting for me to have another breakdown, another mental health crisis and so on. Even though they are a little better now and we don't exactly talk much because they are often judgmental towards me.

Then a few Saturdays ago, me and my other housemate who is probably my best friend to be honest, we were talking about life, how I lost my virginity the day before and we were talking about my ex-partner (who I was still dating at that point). I explained my ex wasn't doing that great because of physical health and a few mental health difficulties.

And my housemate just mentioned in passing something along the lines of "it's difficult when both partners are mentally ill, much less with the same type,".

I was surprised and a little heartbroken at that

comment.

A tiny part of it was because I hate all reminders that my ex-partner was raped repeatedly by their ex-partner. Yet my housemate still fought that I was having a lot of mental health difficulties and I had made no progress in my own healing. That was completely wrong and I don't blame anyone in my social world for thinking this, but it is stupid that my friends have a tendency to think I am always having bad mental health. Even if I don't have a panic attack, anorexia, etc. etc for months.

A final example is possibly my parents because they are always concerned when something bad happens in my life. For example, the breakup with Tokito, something going wrong in the house and a few other things. Maybe they believe that I am only one bad thing away from another mental health crisis.

Of course, I understand that all of this comes from love. My parents and my friends all love me and they want me to be okay. They never want me to be in pain, they don't want me to be suffering and they don't want me to have bad mental health.

Yet it is frustrating that they still think that after at least two or three months of eating okay, after six months of not having any panic attacks or PTSD symptoms and after two or three months of not experiencing social stress because I understand attachment styles now. They all still think I have bad mental health.

I understand why they believe this for another

reason. My housemates and friends were all with me, living with me and seeing the impact first-hand that my rape had on me in terms of mental health. They saw me have breakdowns, they heard me scream at night because of the nightmares and they heard how my PTSD was impacting my life.

All of my housemates also saw my anorexia firsthand too.

This went on for months and months so I understand that me being okay, happy and not having mental health difficulties is basically brand-new to them.

Yet I would appreciate it if they all learnt a little sooner that I was actually okay.

I know my best friend will never believe me when I say I am mentally okay. That just isn't the sort of person they are and that sucks but I know who I am, I know I am okay and I know how to cope if I am not okay. For example, last night at the time of writing, I was so angry with my housemate with OCD because they were micromanaging me and this has been building up for a long time. I can never do anything good enough for them because of their OCD.

Yet instead of letting it destroy my mental health and me starting proper conflict, I removed myself from the situation, I allowed myself to feel my emotions, I practised self-compassion and I cracked on with my night. I did also address the issue with the housemate.

Equally, I know nothing is going to change there because my housemate has no capacity for change when it comes to their OCD.

Over To You As Aspiring or Qualified Psychologists and People

Towards the end of this reflection, I want to highlight that it's important to actually talk to your friend, family member or loved one with the mental health difficulties about how they are actually doing. A lot of my friends and family members that just presume I am fragile with my mental health are going off the "old" me and they aren't willing to have a conversation with me to see why I think I am fine, why I am doing better and how I understand how to cope when something pops up.

A lot of the small instances of disappointment and upset and sadness (maybe even hurt) that my friends cause me to experience could literally be avoided by them taking the time and effort to have a true conversation with me. Instead of just assuming my mental health is bad or them asking in passing.

Of course, as aspiring and qualified psychologists, this is very easy for us to do because for the most part, this is our job. With current and future clients, we are there to have these real conversations and support them with the techniques and tips that we provide them with.

However, we are still friends, children, family members and loved ones. We are still humans after all as I explained in another reflection.

As a result, there might be times when your friend or loved one who's been experiencing mental health difficulties for a long time might say that they are fine and you either don't believe them or you are wary of them saying that. If you have reasons to believe that they aren't as great as they make out then please, don't be annoying and infuriating by just assuming.

Sit down and talk with them, calmly and respectfully and just explain your concerns, why you're wary and just try to become more informed. Try to understand why they believe they're doing great. You might find they've hit a lot of milestones without telling you for one reason or another, but you might be the person who helps them realise they still have progress to make.

Either way is okay.

Communication really is important when dealing with your friends and family members with mental health conditions. You need to respect their needs and boundaries but sometimes the best way to support someone is to gently challenge them.

As hard as that might be.

FOCUS ON THE NEXT DAY AND KEEP YOUR HEAD DOWN

By the time this book comes out, it would have been a while ago that I had a week of increasing trauma responses because me and my partner kissing for the first time (my first kiss ever) brought up a lot of sexual trauma for me. This led to four days of daily crying sessions and I was feeling very overwhelmed and scared that my life was going to return to the hell that was my life pre-specialist-counselling.

However, on the Sunday morning, I was watching some videos from one of my online courses from a business and writing mentor of mine and he mentioned something that I had completely forgotten.

Just focus on the next day, keep your head down and just keep going.

I was watching these videos about six months

late, but at the time of recording, he was going through some really tough business and legal issues because of a foul employee that he had trusted way too much. Him and his wife had been dealing with the business and legal issues all year and it had really impacted them both emotionally, practically and businesswise.

They couldn't do as much charity work as they normally did, they couldn't write as much as they used to and they were having to jump from sorting out one disaster to another.

However, as my business mentor mentioned, when you're dealing with so many other issues that it's stopping you from doing what you love, it's impacting your mental health and it's draining you. In these sort of situations, it is best to focus on the next day.

Don't focus on next week, two days' time or next month. Just focus on one day at a time and one day, things will be better, your life will be easier and whatever life roll you're dealing with, it will pass.

I completely agree.

How Does This Apply To Aspiring and Qualified Psychologists?

This has a lot of parallels for us aspiring and qualified psychologists, because there will be times during our psychology journey that life takes over and it stops us in our tracks. This might be the unfortunate death of a loved one, us not being able to get the clinical psychology work experience or maybe we didn't get the assistant psychologist position that we desperately wanted.

Then there are other factors too that are more serious life roles. For example, experiencing psychological trauma, needing to take time out of university and psychology work, caring for a loved one and so on.

All these different life roles can cause our mental health to dip and for us to slow our psychology journey down so we aren't progressing as quickly as we want to.

When this happens, this can be soul destroying because we've all been working so hard to become a clinical or another type of applied psychologist that when life throws a curveball, it can feel like we will never achieve our goals. Our dreams are shattered, we've failed and we will never ever become a clinical psychologist.

I know several times in my psychology journey, I have truly believed there was no hope at all for me to become a qualified psychologist.

The first time was probably around August 2023 when I had my breakdown because of my homophobic upbringing and child abuse. My mental health was constantly bad, and I was depressed, anxious and I hated myself more than anything. I didn't think I could ever work with others to improve their mental health because my own was so bad.

Yet it passed and my mental health improved.

The only other major time I can remember is

during the seven months after my rape because I was constantly having panic attacks, depression, intense anxiety and a whole bunch of other PTSD reactions. I couldn't even listen to anything mental health-related otherwise I would have a mental health crisis myself.

It was a living nightmare, and going to sleep was even worse.

I never got a break from my mental health.

Yet, it passed and my mental health improved.

And even a few days ago at the time of writing, when my trauma responses were reactivated and I was terrified that my mental health and life would return to those first seven months after my rape. I truly believed that I wouldn't be able to be a clinical psychologist because it was clear my trauma was still impacting me.

Yet after four days, I was okay and my mental health improved.

My point is that even if you don't experience trauma during your clinical psychology journey, there will be times when you don't think you could ever be a psychologist. Maybe you get a bad grade on an assignment, maybe you need to take care of a loved one or maybe you experience a death in the family.

You need to do what's best for you at that moment in time.

If you need to take time out of your psychology journey then please do it. You are the most important person, so please look after yourself.

And during these difficult times, focus on getting

to the next day, then the day after that and the day after that. One day, your mental health and/ or whatever you are going through will get better and you can continue your clinical psychology journey that way.

Chances are at the end of whatever you're going through, you will actually be better off because you have extra experience that other people won't have. And one day, you might meet a client that would appreciate having that shared experience more than you ever know.

It is possible.

So when you're struggling and a life roll stops or bends or delays your psychology journey, please focus on the next day and go going forward.

As hard as that might be in practise.

Here are some questions to help you at the end of this chapter:

- When your mental health dips because something in your psychology journey didn't go to plan, do you feel like your low mood is going to last forever?
- How could you remind yourself in these times that tomorrow might be better?
- What self-care ideas could you use when your mental health dips?

THERE COMES A POINT WHEN TRIGGER IS THE WRONG WORD

In the past few volumes of my *Clinical Psychology Reflections*, there has been a large focus on psychotherapy and trauma because of my child abuse and my rape. I've reflected on a lot of other concepts and facts too, but I wanted to explore something I realised last night.

The Seed

The seed of this reflection was planted in November 2024 when my rape counsellor mentioned how trigger was the wrong word for what happened after a particular day, because my mental health was a lot better, my trauma responses had decreased tons and my PTSD symptoms had greatly reduced in intensity. Instead, she preferred the term "reminder" and at the time, I didn't really think too much of it. I saw and understood what she was saying but the gravity of her wisdom didn't really hit me until last night in June 2025.

It took me seven months to truly realise what she was talking about.

Context

For more recent context, last night I decided to watch another episode of the new series of Doctor Who. The episode was called "Lucky Day" and I won't give away too much of the plot, but as a rape survivor, there were two things that really bothered me.

Firstly, the boyfriend of the main character lied about who he was, what his goals were and what he wanted from the woman. This really bothered and bugged me because this was similar to my rape. The guy had lied, hidden information and he had manipulated me on his profile so he could lure me into a position to rape me.

The episode struck too close to home there in a very innocent and subtle way. I know that was not the vibe the episode was going for in the slightest.

Secondly, because the boyfriend of the main character was deluded as hell. He was very angry and questioned and accused the main character and UNIT (United Nations Intelligence Taskforce- a bit of nerdy lore for you) of lying about aliens and everything and it was a whacky thing to believe considering the in-universe lore.

Anyway, I didn't realise at the time that this bothered me a lot because to me as a rape survivor, there was the objective truth that in Doctor Who, aliens are real and UNIT is protecting the world from them in addition to the Doctor and his companion.

That is the objective truth. Similar to the objective truth that I was raped.

However, people do not always accept the objective truth. For example, there are people that do not believe that vaccines save lives, there are people who do not believe we landed on the moon and so on.

After my rape, certain important others questioned whether I was raped or not. These certain people did not allow me to say I was raped, they denied I was raped and they didn't want to hear what had happened to me.

As a result, when I saw that the boyfriend of the main character was saying that the objective truth was a lie and the main character was making everything up as an attention seeker. I was not happy and this really bothered me.

The Reflection Itself

On the whole, watching this episode brought up a lot of trauma "triggers" or "reminders" to be honest. After watching the episode, I sort of felt that something was wrong and I did some stuff and still felt like something was wrong. I practised about four different self-soothing techniques and I allowed myself to feel my emotions and process what I was feeling and why. I spent a good ten minutes doing this and I thought I was okay.

I would like to admit that this was an isolated incident but back in April, when I was reading a really sweet book *I Want To Kiss You in Public* by Zelda French, there's a scene when it seems that the love interest has lied to the main character in a very, very major way and this really "triggered" or "reminded" me of my rape.

I experienced a good few trauma responses and I couldn't sleep that night.

Last night, I went upstairs to do some reading because I want to finish a really good romantic suspense book (it's *The Coffee Bomb and the Corporate Spy* by Kari Kilgore in case you're interested) and my mind kept shifting back to the episode of Doctor Who, how the boyfriend had lied and it bothered me.

So much so that I couldn't really sleep last night. I had some of the flashbacks, some of the physical sensations and I felt like my rapist was touching me and the like. I haven't experienced these sort of sensations and trauma responses for months.

In the end, I knew I couldn't sleep so I wanted to try a little trick by staying up until I felt tired again. I know grabbing my laptop and doing some light business work for another 40 minutes was not ideal because of the blue light but I wanted to be productive until I was tired again.

Nonetheless, before I went upstairs to read I realised that saying the episode of Doctor Who "triggered" me was wrong. Since I wasn't having the panic attacks, the intense shaking and the crippling feeling of dread and like I was about to die or be raped again like I was during the worst of my PTSD.

I was uncomfortable and I was really bothered by that episode but I was not triggered. I was having barely any PTSD symptoms and trauma responses in comparison to the past.

That's why I argue that saying or thinking that I was "triggered" is a disservice to everything I have overcome and just how much progress I have made since my rape. Also, I strongly believe that saying I was "triggered" risks worsening my mental health overall because I might sadly start to believe that I will never escape my rape, it will always control me and there is no hope for me amongst all the other depressing and anxious thoughts and lies that my mind tried to convince me of months ago.

In reality, I was not "triggered" and I have made amazing progress so this is why I think for all trauma survivors, there comes a point where trigger is the wrong word. Since trigger ignores the great progress our clients have made, it ignores their strength and their resilience and how amazing they are doing right now in the present.

Instead I think the word "reminder" is sort of better but even for what happened last night, it didn't really remind me of my rape. Sportswear used to be a good reminder of my rape because I was raped in sportswear, the gym and the smell of sweat was another effective reminder of my rape because of its association with sportswear and attractive guys.

Yet last night was not a "reminder".

Perhaps, it's better that I think of it as a "bother" or an "uncomfortable feeling" because that is more what it is. And I actually quite like those words because these words don't minimise the great progress I've made, they don't take any power away from me and they describe my lack of trauma responses.

There are always certain things in life that make us uncomfortable, bug us and bother us and these things can harm our mental health at times. Yet we still feel uncomfortable for a while then we move on, enjoy life and deal with the uncomfortable feeling.

It doesn't have any power over us for the long term and I'm okay about that.

The Meaning of This Reflection

Ultimately, this reflection was about showing you, as an aspiring or qualified psychologist, that our words have power and even how we decide to describe something with our client has the power to impact their perceptions about their experiences, themselves and their progress.

Just think about your words, your client's words and maybe talk to them about their perceptions and their word usage when appropriate. We're used to doing this as part of the cognitive approach because we work to challenge a client's biased cognitive processes and perceptions of events.

Let's go one step further after the most intense part of the trauma work is done. Let's never take our eyes off the ball when it comes to word use when talking about events and moments related to traumatic experiences.

IMPORTANCE OF VALIDATING OTHERS AND MY LITTLE SOCIAL EXPERIMENT

For the past four days, I've been running a little social experiment and it has been going amazingly well.

Since the whole drama of the last reflection, I don't know what made me want to focus on it, but I wanted to focus on validating other people. I know from my personal experience how important being validated and supported is and I wanted to become better at it myself.

I am going to write an episode of The Psychology World Podcast this week on how validation is a superpower in social communication. This book shouldn't be coming out until 2026 so this episode will be 334 of The Psychology World Podcast.

In this reflection, I'll explain what is validation, why is it important in your personal life and your clinical psychology life and how my little experiment has been working.

It will be a lot of fun.

What is Validation?

According to Rathus and Miller (2015) validation is when you understand where the other person is coming from and you don't have to agree with what they have done or what they've said. As well as validation involves recognising someone's feelings and thoughts make sense given the situation and their life circumstances.

Also if you show that you acknowledge and understand their feelings then it shows to the other person that we are listening without judgment and with empathy. This is flat out critical for building a stronger relationship in therapy. As well as validating other people, especially in therapy, can be difficult because we want to validate what they are saying, but not always their actions.

Why Is Validation Important In Therapy?

I've already mentioned briefly why validation is important because it allows you to build a stronger therapeutic relationship with the client. Yet based on my personal experience as a rape survivor who was experiencing depression, Post-Traumatic Stress Disorder, anxiety and later anorexia. I was in such a bad place that it was so nice, so heartwarming and kind to be validated.

Especially, when in my life no one else was validating me. The social environment that I lived in before I moved in with my best friend at that time always invalidated me. They flat out couldn't understand my panic attacks, my distress and my rape triggers. So they would blame me for my rape, they would shout and berate me for my mental health.

I still remember them saying that my rape was a well-deserved lesson.

Therefore, to have someone, a stranger, validate me for a change was amazing. It was so kind and nice and it really improved my mental health for a moment. It helped me not feel like I was going insane.

In addition, when it came to my anorexia when I was losing a kilogram a week, I was constantly tired, I was feeling sick constantly and I was refusing to eat. I remember a few times when I had panic attacks when I smelt food and I was happily going without eating for 24 or 25 hours. Medical professionals and my rape counsellor at the time invalidated me.

They didn't believe I had anorexia.

I looked fine despite my dramatic weight loss and psychological symptoms of anorexia. They completely invalidated me.

In fact, there was only one person saying I had anorexia and they were right, but everyone else was invalidating me.

As a result, when my anorexia counsellor validated me, it was a great feeling. And it really helped us to form the therapeutic relationship that helped me to change my life for the better.

Validating other people can be an amazingly powerful tool in therapy.

How Can Validation Help Your Personal Life?

As a result of my child abuse, I have disorganised attachment. This means I have anxious attachment and avoidant attachment depending on the person and I can switch between them very easily. Thankfully, I have done a lot of work and I have a much more secure attachment style now and I find social relationships a lot easier and more enjoyable because I am no longer anxious and constantly stressed about being abandoned.

However, a trait of avoidant people is they always focus on solutions because they don't want to deal with the conflict or emotions of the other person. They avoid them instead. As well as anxiously attached people tend to accidentally get so focused on their own feelings of overwhelm, anxiety and fear of abandonment that the other person's feelings get missed.

This is always by accident but it doesn't help secure attachment form.

Moreover, I told you in the last reflection about how horrible it felt when Jane invalidated my fun, joyful moment about the laser pointer. I felt sad, I felt shut down, and it really did harm our friendship. We don't have a friendship anymore and my mental health, my stress levels and I am doing a lot better now.

It was the right decision for me.

Furthermore, on Tuesday, on the way back from an Outreach event in London (we never ever tend to work in London), me and another ambassador who I'm friends with outside of work, were catching up because we haven't seen each other for a good month or two. And we were talking about Oliver and Jane and something deeply disturbing about Oliver that has upset me and I need to process it because it is morally and ethically insane and it could be borderline illegal.

And I mentioned how after my rape and when my mental health was at its worst, I was dependent on Oliver for a lot of support. And instead of judging me, berating me or saying I was silly for being dependent on Oliver, the other ambassador simply said *that's understandable*. That small talk of validation really relaxed me and it allowed us to continue the lovely conversation we were having.

This other ambassador isn't the sort of friend I could call on if I had a problem, she isn't someone I would go out of my way to see but when we get together, we get on great and we like talking to each other.

It was a brilliant 50-minute train ride.

Therefore, if you want to be more secure, I highly recommend validating the feelings and thoughts of your friends.

The results of my little experiment supports this

point even more.

What Was My Little Social Experiment?

Validating others is a learnt skill. It is something that needs to be practised and over time, if you practise it enough, it can become an automatic thing. Therefore, for the past four days, I have been practising it and being mindful of validating others.

Thankfully, I have had a lot of social opportunities to be able to test this experiment out on. I have had Oliver, I have had a lot of Outreach work this week and I have been driving ambassadors across the county to help them out.

I have done so much talking this week and I have loved it.

My experiment was how would validating others make me feel and how would it improve my social relationships.

The results were it would make myself and the other person feel good, it led to better, more fulfilling conversations and it was just lovely.

On Monday, I worked with a wonderful woman from Outreach who mainly does the Post-16 programmes and both of us love working together. She finds me a pleasure and a reassuring presence with my enthusiasm (that was a paraphrased version of some feedback I got today). And she mentioned Oliver was doing a good job in this longer-term programme that she runs.

I told Oliver this later that night when I got home and he thanked me but he was unsure because he doesn't feel like he's doing a good job because he isn't the best ambassador. I could have dismissed his concerns and skip straight to me being supportive, but I wanted to practise validating him.

I said something along the following: "I get that because I know you find it hard talking to students and there are more experienced ambassadors. But from my point of view, you have really improved in the last year and you will continue to improve over time,"

I said more than that but that was the general gist, and Oliver appreciated it and he explained more about how he was feeling about Outreach work and how he didn't feel like he was the best at it. It was a lovely conversation that I doubt would have been as nice if I hadn't validated him first.

I wish I could do an explanation and give examples of me validating people for each day of this week so far. I know I have examples but I have done so much talking with so many different people that I can't remember them. I am a little tired as well.

However, I know that validating me has made other people smile, thank yous and it has led to other deeper conversations that both of us have enjoyed.

The only other validation experience I remember is me talking to a friend of me because she messaged devastated, really depressed and upset because she sadly got rejected for some funding for her PhD. She was gutted and I wanted to support her and suggest solutions but I couldn't invalidate her feelings.

Also, she was talking about not working this weekend at an event she normally loves because she felt too depressed and upset to interact with others.

This is what I sent her instead:

I know there have been days when any sort of Ambassador work just wasn't right for me and I've definitely benefited from staying home as I felt with whatever I was dealing with. Yet sometimes when I've been devastated and not the best, open days were great to help me feel better. I understand both choices.

Message me if you need anything. I'm always here for you. I'm working a lot of Outreach this week but if you want to meet up for dinner or a coffee so you can talk. I'm happy to.

Here, I wanted to strike a balance between validating her feelings and suggesting an alternative course of action that might help her. She was super grateful and she was really happy with my messages.

Overall, at the end of this reflection, I hope you're starting to understand the importance of validating others in terms of their mental health and in your personal life. Validating others really can be a social superpower that can make other people like, appreciate you and know that you are an amazing and empathetic person who they can share things with.

Validating sometimes might make you and them feel better, it might make them like you more and sometimes it might lead to better, deeper conversations revealing information and friendships that you never thought possible.

Clinical Psychology Reference

Rathus, J. H., & Miller, A. L. (2015). DBT®skills manual for adolescents. The Guilford Press.

REDUCING UNCERTAINITY AT DIAGNOSIS FOR FRIENDS AND FAMILY

Last week at my university, my Clinical Psychology MSc was having their first-ever clinical psychology research conference where MSc students could present their research. It turned out a lot of people wanted me to present either because they found my research fascinating or because they really like me as a speaker.

Personally, I have no idea what they hear when I speak but I appreciate the sheer confidence they have in me. I am not an amazing speaker.

Anyway, there were a lot of different phrases, little ideas and little arguments that I wrote down because I wanted to reflect on them. The idea that we need to reduce uncertainty at diagnosis for family and carers is a very interesting idea that I want to reflect more on.

Originally, the idea came from a Parkinson's presentation and the young woman presented made a point about when a loved one is diagnosed with Parkinson's Disease, the carer and family are very nervous, concerned and they have no idea what happens next.

Of course, the doctor, mental health professional or whatever healthcare professional is doing the diagnosis talks and provides the person with dementia with resources. Yet the carer and the family is an afterthought according to this young woman's research.

This is why I really like the holistic approach to working because a mental health condition, or in this case a neurodegenerative condition, does not only impact the person themselves. All mental health conditions impact the person's social network, and this includes the person's carers, family and loved ones.

It is the carers and family members who are going to be doing the majority of the caring responsibilities anyway. As a result, the mental health condition, in this case Parkinson's, will have a massive impact on them.

To see a metaphor from the systemic school of thought within mental health, when someone has a mental health condition or a neurodegenerative condition, it creates a ricochet effect across the entire family system, so it impacts everyone.

Another way to explain the impact of dementia or Parkinson's is imagine a glassy lake and someone throws a stone in (this represents the diagnosis) and you see the ripples travel for ages across the entire surface of the lake.

This is exactly how a Parkinson's diagnosis impacts an entire social network, whether we realise it or not.

As a result, as aspiring or qualified mental health professionals, we need to be aware that whenever we diagnose someone. We need to not only give information about the treatment, symptoms and more about the mental health condition to the person with the condition, but those around them too.

I will caveat this by saying, unless it is a neurodegenerative condition, it is important we only share this information if the client wants it. For example, when I went for my anorexia counselling, yes, my anorexia was having a massive negative impact on my friends, my family and other aspects of my social network but I wouldn't have wanted them to be told everything.

I would have liked the freedom to drip-feed them information about how bad my health was over time. This would have prevented them from getting overwhelmed, them getting even more stressed and them pestering me.

Equally, I think it would have been lovely if my counsellor had given me some kind of resource to give my housemates, because these were the main people who saw the impact of my anorexia and how bad my health was. If they had had some kind of resource, information or actual knowledge about anorexia, then maybe they wouldn't have pestered me as much or maybe they would have managed the entire situation better.

My housemates did make some critical mistakes that really hurt me, distressed me and harmed our relationship. Even though anorexia does that on its own.

Anyway, when it comes to Parkinson's or other neurodegenerative conditions, it's important to think about the carers and family members too. Since a diagnosis confirms their worst fears, their stressors and it confirms that their life will never be the same again.

Their partner's, husband's or wife's memory or physical symptoms weren't *just* another part of getting older. They are going to get a lot, lot worse before sadly, they pass away and that means their life changes forever. All those happy plans of future trips, future evening snuggled up together on the sofa and all those happy plans of future grandchildren.

All gone in an instant.

That's why we need to provide support for carers and families, and that's all before we consider the physical, mental and emotional toll of looking after someone with dementia or Parkinson's for the rest of their lives.

It's hard.

My great-aunt is a superhero for managing as well as she did for all those years, even though it made her into a hermit that didn't know how to go outside and live her own life by the time my Great-uncle died three years ago.

This is why I really appreciate, admire and respect what the Parkinson's centre at my university does. The centre offers counselling, support groups and socials for the spouses and carers of people with Parkinson's. This helps maintain the mental health of the carers too.

Another critical aspect of Parkinson's care.

You cannot expect the people with Parkinson's to have excellent care if their home and social support network is burnt out or dealing with negative mental health.

This is why a holistic approach at diagnosis is critical, so we can support families, support the person with the mental health condition and ensure everyone thrives in the end and can support each other.

There is no one person impacted by mental health. Mental health impacts everyone, whether you have a condition or not.

LOOKING AT FRIENDS AND FAMILY IN MENTAL HEALTH RESEARCH

Another research presentation was done by someone who wasn't a clinical psychology masters student, instead they were studying intellectual disabilities at the university and she did her research on staff wellbeing and mental health in a charity. Yet what's interesting isn't the presentation itself, it was a comment afterwards made by my programme director.

My programme director touched on the student's off-the-cuff comment about wanting to research or use the staff's friends and family in the research. Yet because of time constraints and all the other problems the student faced, because it turns out wanting to do research in a real-world company takes so much longer than everyone thinks it will. She wasn't able to research the friends and family.

Personally, I flat out loved the idea of including friends and family in mental health research, because instead of simply testing the participant themselves with self-reported measures. For instance, they might say their mental health is improving, they feel calmer and happier in general. Friends and family are independent and they can add their thoughts.

Why Might This Be Important?

I think this is important for a few reasons. Firstly, self-reported data can be biased because of social desirability, the person might want to appear to have better mental health than they actually do amongst other factors. Friends and family observations and data is a good way to get round this issue.

Secondly, if your boss asks you to take part in a mental health study, even if you're familiar with research practices. How can you be 100% sure your boss will never see your individual results? You can't. Also, if your workplace is a little backstabby, if your organisation is looking to make cuts and if you don't get on great with your manager. If you're stressed about work and you already have some negative mental health, are you really going to risk being honest in a mental health study?

Are you really going to risk showing that your mental health isn't great?

And even more importantly, are you really going to risk your job? Especially, when you have bills to pay and maybe a family, a partner or children to support.

No, you aren't. This is why you might subtly, even without knowing change your responses in the mental health research.

Thirdly, the mental health intervention might improve your work mental health really well. You might be happier, you might feel more relaxed, less anxious and more competent at work. The mental health study results might reflect that improvement significantly. Yet that doesn't mean, your mental health is great at home and if the intervention isn't leading to a better wellbeing outcome at home then this is something the researchers might need to investigate.

This is where friends and family can be useful. They are outside of the workplace (you can have friends at work but I'm ignoring them in this reflection) so they can tell the researchers if their loved one or friend is improving outside of work too.

In addition, friends and family can tell researchers if the mental health intervention is having any unintended consequences too.

For example, I always remember in the Applied Psychology module in the final year of my undergraduate degree, we learnt about transformational leadership. It was a brilliant type of leadership that led to major improvements in workplace wellbeing, productivity and the workers were really happy. Yet there was a problem.

Two or three years later, people's sick days skyrocketed because they were working themselves so hard because they were enjoying their job and the leadership was being so inspiring. They were making themselves sick and burning out because of it.

As a result, if the workers in your mental health study are coming home, fatigued, short-tempered or just not interested in doing anything pleasurable outside of work. Then the friends and family members should definitely tell the researchers and this negative impact on home life should be investigated and acknowledged too.

Just something to think about.

Finally, looking at friends and family might be important because of method triangulation. This is where you use multiple research methods to back up your conclusions. Let's say you're doing quantitative surveys and mental health scales with participants at work to investigate the impact of your 12-week intervention. Perhaps conduct semi-structured interviews with friends and family members to see the impact of the intervention too on their loved ones.

Always try to think about other ways to support your data, arguments and conclusions.

Personal Reaction To This Idea

Personally, back in 2023 when I was originally designing my study on the mental health implications of gender-affirming clothing on transgender young adults. I wanted to include interviews with friends and family members so they could confirm the young person's mental health improved when they started wearing gender-affirming clothing.

In the end, I didn't add that part of the methodology because it would have been too intense and difficult but it was still interesting and it would have been useful information.

I never really thought about interviewing friends or family members for any of my other transgender mental health studies. Even though, I just realised it might have been useful to interview some friends, partners and loved ones in my chosen name study about the strategies transgender people used to pick their chosen names. That would have been useful, but at least the study turned out great anyway.

Conclusion

Ultimately, at the end of this reflection, I want to say that whenever we conduct research, we should always think broader and wider than we originally do. We need to think about how best to back up our results, our conclusions and our data. Method triangulation is a great way to do that and a part of this can be talking, interviewing and researching the friends and family of our participants.

Our participant's friends and family are a lot more likely to know our participants, including their opinions, their thoughts, their mental health, than we ever will. So why are we ignoring them in our research? Why aren't we regularly tapping into this potential goldmine of data?

Of course, friends and family members will bring their own biases, reasons and blind spots to our research, but they will add a lot of depth and richness too.

Just something to think about.

SOME TRAINEE CLINICAL PSYCHOLOGISTS MIGHT PREFER AI AVATARS AND BENEFIT MORE FROM THEM

Towards the beginning of the book, I wrote a few reflections just after taking part in some studies on using artificial intelligence in clinical psychology training. One of the research talks at the clinical psychology research conference was the results of that study.

A lot of the findings agreed and backed up with what I already discussed in those reflections, but there was a single line in my notes that really surprised me.

Some people prefer AI training tools and might benefit more from them compared to roleplays.

I want to reflect on this because I was shocked.

Personally, I think I was shocked because I was surprised some people preferred awkwardly talking to an AI Chatbot or avatar compared to roleplays. As well as some people would prefer to only use AI training tools.

Let's look at the arguments for this comment.

I understand the AI training tools might be better in certain aspects compared to roleplays. Since AI avatars and chatbots are programmed to not reveal too much information to the psychologist conducting the psychological assessment, exactly how less-than-forthcoming clients are in the real world. This means AI tools are brilliant for helping a trainee psychologist to develop those skills for use in the real world.

You could argue AI training tools are better than roleplays for teaching psychologists how to get information from a quieter client.

In addition, you could argue that AI training tools are better than roleplays because the issue with roleplays are both of you are trainee clinical psychologists. You both know what you want to achieve, you want both of you to be comfortable and because you're already in the same cohort together and roleplays tend to be done in friendship groups. You already know the person, you might have a friendship or rapport with them.

Even though I didn't have too many friends in my cohort, I still always had fun and there was nothing really professional and hardcore about the roleplays I did during my clinical psychology MSc.

As a result of the AI training tools never having met you before, the training tools are useful to help you develop the skills of client engagement.

However, roleplays have something that AI training tools will never have. They have the human factor, the human connection and because roleplays involve real humans, they will always be better at creating and training those human, interpersonal skills that therapists need.

AI training tools might be good at teaching the clinical skills.

Roleplays will always be best for teaching the interpersonal skills.

In addition, in my experience, AI training tools lack the humanity, their facial expressions, their emotional tone and they don't have a background. That all impacts the reliability and validity of a psychological assessment.

We know from personal experience, research and listening to our lecturers that childhood experiences, interpersonal relationships and where we live and where we are from can all impact our mental health. Yet an AI training tool will never be able to cover the full depth and breadth of human experiences that can be critical in filling out a clinical formulation and psychological assessment.

I remember I kept trying to ask the AI avatar where their culture and country of origin was, because I wanted to identify some Core Beliefs, Rules to Live By, impact of childhood experiences and some protective factors we could use in therapeutic work moving forward. Yet the AI avatar didn't know so this entire social aspect of an assessment was missed.

That is really bad.

The closest I got to any social aspect in the assessment was the AI avatar saying how they isolated themselves from friends, they didn't go out much and that was it.

Nothing like a real psychological assessment.

Personally, I would be interested in talking to the participants who preferred AI training tools to roleplays to see if there were any other factors at play. For example, is it possible that certain students prefer the AI training tools out of fear of judgment or failure? In a classroom environment, they might feel a need to compete, to prove to their friends and others that they know what they're doing and that they would be a good clinical psychologist in the future.

If you make a mistake in front of your friends, your classmates or a judgmental person in a roleplay then they might remember, and tease you about it.

Equally, you might perceive them to be judging you because of your own self-doubt about whether you have the skills or experience to become a clinical psychologist. When in reality, they didn't even notice or they just laughed about it because we all have to start from somewhere.

An AI training tool wouldn't remember the mistake you made.

In addition, I would be interested in seeing if this is a social comparison thing. If you're doing roleplays with your cohort you're nervous, you aren't sure what to do and you're scared about how you word your questions and whether your questions would actually be appropriate in the real world. Then you overhear or see someone else effortlessly doing a better job than you. You aren't going to feel great, are you?

You don't get that pressure or social comparison with an AI training tool.

Ultimately, at the end of this reflection, I want to stress again that I do not believe AI training tools should ever take over roleplays in clinical psychology training. There might be some benefits over AI training tools over roleplays but roleplays can still teach us a lot of critical skills in becoming a clinical psychologist.

And if you do prefer the sound of AI training tools over roleplays and even, vice versa, ask yourself why. Does it come from fear or another reason?

Just something to think about.

THINKING ABOUT LYING, AGE AND SYMPTOMS

The penultimate research talk at the clinical psychology research conference was done by a MSc cognitive psychology student. She was a little too uptight for my personal tastes but her research was really interesting and her presentation could have been a little more engaging and interpersonal, instead of being spoken down to. Yet there was still some information I wanted to reflect on.

The basic premise of her research was how lying behaviour changes across the lifespan. She looked at lying in younger adults and older adults to see how lying behaviour increases or decreases. Her results showed that as we age, our lying behaviour becomes less effective and it becomes harder to create more complex lies because several cognitive functions decrease.

I talk more about this in my book, *How Does Ageing Affect Us?* Available wherever you bought this book from.

In addition, as this was a clinical psychology research conference, she applied her findings to mental health settings. She proposed that there's a link between mental health symptoms and lying behaviour based on her experience as a social support worker as she was accused of stealing when she hadn't by someone with dementia.

This is a rather common and distressing experience for nurses, support workers and other professionals who interact with people with neurodegenerative conditions.

Before we explore the clinical psychology implications of thinking about older adults, lying behaviours and how symptoms of mental health conditions can impact unintentional lying behaviour. I want to give you a brief bit of context first of all by showing you some information about how lying behaviour evolves across the lifespan.

Here are some extracts from my book, *Forensic Psychology of Deception*. Available wherever you bought this book from.

"Why Is The Lying Of Young Children Naive?

Compared to the lying of older children and adults, the lying behaviours of young children are rather naïve. Since the lying of older children is more complex and more "knowing", and older children lie for a wide range of different reasons and like adults, older children lie to serve themselves.

However, this is much harder for young people to develop. Since it isn't until the age of four that children develop Theory of Mind so young children assume that their parents will take whatever they say literally and instantly understand what they mean. At this point in their lives, young children don't understand that their parents or caregivers will probably have a different perspective.

This connects to one of my favourite topics in developmental psychology and this is egocentrism. Since young children aren't able to take other viewpoints and they can only focus on their own personal rewards, punishments, goals as well as dreams. They don't understand other people's reactions or aren't "able to put themselves in their shoes".

On the whole, it's important to realise here that young children can't understand the concept or value of "white lies" and how they can help protect another person's emotional welfare.

Equally, there is a benefit to young children being egocentric. The benefit is they can be awful liars because they don't understand or care to learn about the times, places and ways to make a lie successful. As well as young children don't realise the importance of hiding their true feelings by covering their tracks.

Like I should have done when I was really young.

What About The Lying Behaviour Of Older Children?

Nonetheless, when the child gets older, their lying behaviour becomes more and more like their parents because they learn from getting trapped by their parents' teaching them how honesty is the best policy and the times when the older child has tried to hide the truth from their parents.

Furthermore, older children become more "cognitively able" to copy and learn from their parents' lying behaviour. As a result, if we care to indulge the idea that lying is a skill (which I personally think it is, whether that is right or wrong is another debate entirely) then it's like a child's lying skill matures as they age. This helps to make the older child as effective at lying as their caregiver, who is often hypocritical.

How Does Lying Becomes More Complex In A Social World?

Another reason why lying becomes more complex and "improves" is because we live in a socially interdependent world so children do grow past the normal developmental stage of self-absorption. This leads to older children being better at telling lies, and it improves their ability to mirror their parents' motives.

In other words, the reasons for the lying becomes more polished, mature and complex.

For instance, when children are young, they lie to get what they want so they might lie to fulfil an emotional need or a physical one. This happens because as you can expect, children have no authority so they are completely dependent on the caregiver.

Therefore, young children need to find ways to incentivise their parents to give them what they need.

However, as the child ages and their cognitions and understanding becomes more complex, their motives become more complex too.

As a result, children are able to lie more tactically and more manipulatively if required."

Thinking About Lying, Age and Symptoms In Mental Health Settings

The reason why I wanted to reflect on this woman's research is because she mentioned that support workers and other individuals, including friends as well as family members, should be given education about how symptoms impact lying behaviour. Also, they should be educated about lying in older age because whenever we think about lying, we tend to think it doesn't change.

Her research shows the opposite.

Lies in older adults are less imaginative, more difficult and more cognitively demanding because of the neurodegeneration in the brain. Therefore, professionals in healthcare settings should become more aware of this fact because unlike younger adults who have the cognitive ability to lie for personal gain, manipulation and to get others in trouble, older adults are less able to.

Of course, as I talk about in my Ageing book, there will be older adults who have remarkably intact cognitive processes, so their lying abilities will match or even exceed younger adults.

Generally speaking, that is not the case.

In addition, support workers and other healthcare professionals who work with people with neurodegenerative conditions should be made aware that if their client makes an accusation that they stole from them. This isn't the older person being evil, harsh or wanting to cause trouble. This is an example of the cognitive symptom that their condition is causing them.

The older adult in their confused state truly believes that you stole from them, so this isn't a lie to them. This isn't even deception as defined in my book *Forensic Psychology of Deception*. They believe they're telling the truth so we need to be mindful of these factors.

Both from a healthcare perspective so we can investigate or deal with these accusations however the healthcare setting deems fit. Yet also from the perspective of the healthcare workers themselves, because to be accused by someone you're caring for, looking after and supporting. That is very distressing and you're likely to want to distance yourself from that client and you'll be worried about your job.

Healthcare workers need to bear in mind this is nothing against them, and this is a symptom of their neurodegenerative condition.

On the other hand, you do hear stories about healthcare workers stealing, financially abusing and manipulating their clients. This happens in the real world, so we can't take these research findings to the extreme by not believing any accusations made by older adults. Otherwise, there is a risk, financial, emotional and other forms of abuse might thrive more than they already do.

Ultimately, at the end of this reflection, we need to be mindful of how lying behaviour changes as we age, but also the cognitive decline seen in pathological ageing can impact lying behaviour. Possibly leading to false accusations.

Ideally, now we know this research finding, we might be able to go further and explore how do lies induced by pathological ageing differ from lies induced by the older adult wanting to deceive.

I have no idea how you would research it but it's interesting food for thought for sure.

THERE HAS TO BE MORE THAN MEDICATION IN APPOINTMENTS AND CREATING A PATIENT CONCERN INVENTORY

The final research talk I want to reflect on in these pages was about Parkinson's disease, and the young woman presenting it was talking about how whenever people with Parkinson's Disease come to a medical appointment. They might have concerns about their sleep, their mood, their mental health symptoms, their social functioning and so many more concerns.

The vast majority of clients with any mental health condition, to be honest, have a list of things *they* would like to talk about in a medical appointment even though they only have 15 minutes then they will not have another appointment for 3- to 6-months later.

However, due to the strength and pervasive nature of the biomedical model, all the medical doctors are interested in is talking about medication. How is the person with Parkinson's Disease finding the medication, is it helping, do they need to increase the dosage and more.

The qualitative research in this study showed that clients did not want to talk about medication in their medical appointments. They were actually happy with the medication and what was actually impacting their life, their happiness and causing them distress where other factors that the medical doctor never asked about.

In my experience, medical doctors only ever focus on what they can see with their own eyes or specialist biological tests. They are never interested in how a person is feeling, experiencing chronic pain or forgetfulness or any other psychological impacts of their condition.

For people living with conditions, like Parkinson's, this is not good enough.

Of course, you might argue that it is down to the client to step up, talk about what *they* want to and they should make the medical doctor listen to them. In reality, this is not how it works because medical doctors are powerful and they have the power to give or deny a client treatment if they don't think it is needed.

Also, there is a massive power differential between a medical doctor and a client and so many clients with a neurogenerative condition (or any health conditions for that matter) have experiences of being told that they're overreacting, they don't know what they're talking about and so on.

Medical doctors have silenced them before, so why would this be any different?

You only need to read Miranda Hart's book *I Haven't Been Entirely Honest With You* to see how a medical doctor dismissed her health concerns completely. It later turned out she was far from overreacting because she had Lyme disease.

There has to be more conversation in these short appointments other than medication if we really want to improve the lives, daily functioning and happiness of people living with neurodegenerative conditions.

That's where the Patient Concern Inventory comes in.

What Is The Patient Concern Inventory?

Originally developed in 2009 by Professor Simon Rogers at the Liverpool Head and Neck Centre for outpatient cancer patients. The Patient Concern Inventory is a condition-specific prompt list that covers a range of areas and before an appointment, a patient ticks the areas they are struggling with so they can talk about it and get support in the appointment.

This was found to be a cost-effective intervention, it helped clinician-patient communication and it led to improvements in quality of life.

As a result, the MSc students working on this

project reviewed the literature, interviewed healthcare professionals who had decades of Parkinson's experience between them, and refined and refined and refined the Inventory until they produced one specific for Parkinson's.

They broke down the Inventory into 6 main areas:

- Physical Functioning
- Emotional and psychological wellbeing
- Treatment questions
- Social care and wellbeing
- Activities in daily life
- Multidisciplinary team

This allowed clients with Parkinson's to get this Inventory before their medical appointment, they could review it, tick off symptoms and items they were concerned about. Then when they went into their medical appointment, they would give it to the doctor, the doctor would review it and they would talk about what the client wanted to.

This means the treatment and interventions offered to the client are tailored-made to them, their lives and what is negatively impacting their daily living. This is great news and this is something we should try to do for all mental health and physical conditions.

This decreases the power difference between doctors and clients, it means clients can feel like they're being listened to, respected and they can work with the doctors to solve their difficulties. So they can live a happier, more productive life where they are suffering less.

There has to be more than medication in appointments.

Just remember that.

CONCLUSION

After all 20 of the past clinical psychology reflections, we really have looked at some brilliant topics, and this is why I flat out love these books. These reflections have allowed me to reflect on my toxic living situation, the issues I have with housemates and apply all of this experience in lessons that I can use as an aspiring psychologist.

These reflections have been a space to reflect, to process and to sort through my own thoughts and feelings on these situations and experiences with my housemates. I am not perfect, I am not a God and I am a human that will make mistakes, but as long as I put up boundaries and I live my life by my values then I will be okay.

I know how difficult living in tricky situations can be, and I hope that you now understand how social factors can impact people's mental health.

You can take this knowledge forward in your

own clinical psychology journey.

In addition, these reflections make me focus, listen and look deeper when I'm attending an event like a clinical psychology research conference. To be honest, because I was so busy with my dissertation, my writing and business projects so without these reflections, I probably would not have gone to the conference.

I would have missed out on a lot of great knowledge without these reflections.

Ultimately, I want to give you a massive thank you, dear reader. You buying these books, engaging with my content and helping me to reflect on clinical psychology means the world to me. Without you, I couldn't do what I love so thank you.

Thank you from the bottom of my heart. You're amazing.

I hope you've learnt something from this book and I hope to see you in another clinical psychology reflection book soon.

Have a great day.

https://www.subscribepage.io/psychologyboxset

CHECK OUT THE PSYCHOLOGY WORLD PODCAST FOR MORE PSYCHOLOGY INFORMATION! AVAILABLE ON ALL MAJOR PODCAST APPS.

About the author:

Connor Whiteley is the author of over 60 books in the sci-fi fantasy, nonfiction psychology and books for writer's genre and he is a Human Branding Speaker and Consultant.

He is a passionate warhammer 40,000 reader, psychology student and author.

Who narrates his own audiobooks and he hosts The Psychology World Podcast.

All whilst studying Psychology at the University of Kent, England.

Also, he was a former Explorer Scout where he gave a speech to the Maltese President in August 2018 and he attended Prince Charles' 70th Birthday Party at Buckingham Palace in May 2018.

Plus, he is a self-confessed coffee lover!

<u>All books in 'An Introductory Series':</u>

How To Improve Your Relationships
How Does Ageing Affect Us?
Introduction To Psychotherapies
I Am Not A Victim, I Am A Survivor
Breaking The Silence
Healing As A Survivor
Clinical Psychology and Transgender Clients
Clinical Psychology
Moral Psychology
Myths About Clinical Psychology
401 Statistics Questions For Psychology Students
Careers In Psychology
Psychology of Suicide
Dementia Psychology
Clinical Psychology Reflections Volume 4
Forensic Psychology of Terrorism And Hostage-Taking
Forensic Psychology of False Allegations
Year In Psychology
CBT For Anxiety
CBT For Depression
Applied Psychology
BIOLOGICAL PSYCHOLOGY 3RD EDITION
COGNITIVE PSYCHOLOGY THIRD

EDITION
SOCIAL PSYCHOLOGY- 3RD EDITION
ABNORMAL PSYCHOLOGY 3RD EDITION
PSYCHOLOGY OF RELATIONSHIPS- 3RD EDITION
DEVELOPMENTAL PSYCHOLOGY 3RD EDITION
HEALTH PSYCHOLOGY
RESEARCH IN PSYCHOLOGY
A GUIDE TO MENTAL HEALTH AND TREATMENT AROUND THE WORLD- A GLOBAL LOOK AT DEPRESSION
FORENSIC PSYCHOLOGY
THE FORENSIC PSYCHOLOGY OF THEFT, BURGLARY AND OTHER CRIMES AGAINST PROPERTY
CRIMINAL PROFILING: A FORENSIC PSYCHOLOGY GUIDE TO FBI PROFILING AND GEOGRAPHICAL AND STATISTICAL PROFILING.
CLINICAL PSYCHOLOGY
FORMULATION IN PSYCHOTHERAPY
PERSONALITY PSYCHOLOGY AND INDIVIDUAL DIFFERENCES
CLINICAL PSYCHOLOGY REFLECTIONS VOLUME 1

Other books by Connor Whiteley:

The Death of Graham Adams
Bearing Witness
The Twelve
The Wrong Body
The Assassination Of Bettie English
Wining And Dying
Eight Hours
Uniformed Cabal
A Case Most Christmas

Gay Romance Novellas

Breaking, Nursing, Repairing A Broken Heart
Jacob And Daniel
Fallen For A Lie
Spying And Weddings
Clean Break
Awakening Love
Meeting A Country Man
Loving Prime Minister
Snowed In Love
Never Been Kissed
Love Betrays You
Love And Hurt

Lord of War Origin Trilogy:

Not Scared Of The Dark
Madness

Burn Them All

<u>Way Of The Odyssey</u>
Odyssey of Rebirth
Convergence of Odysseys
Odyssey Of Hope
Odyssey of Enlightenment

<u>Lady Tano Fantasy Adventure Stories</u>
Betrayal
Murder
Annihilation
Rising Shadow
Coming of Demons

<u>Agents of The Emperor</u>
Deceitful Terra
Blood And Wrath
Infiltration
Fuel To The Fire
Return of The Ancient Ones
Vigilance
Angels of Fire
Kingmaker
The Eight
The Lost Generation
Hunt

Emperor's Council
Speaker of Treachery
Birth Of The Empire
Terraforma
Spaceguard

The Rising Augusta Fantasy Adventure Series
Rise To Power
Rising Walls
Rising Force
Rising Realm

The Fireheart Fantasy Series
Heart of Fire
Heart of Lies
Heart of Prophecy
Heart of Bones
Heart of Fate

City of Assassins (Urban Fantasy)
City of Death
City of Martyrs
City of Pleasure
City of Power

Lord Of War Trilogy (Agents of The Emperor)
Not Scared Of The Dark
Madness
Burn It All Down

Miscellaneous:
Dead Names
RETURN
FREEDOM
SALVATION
Reflection of Mount Flame
The Masked One
The Great Deer
English Independence

OTHER SHORT STORIES BY CONNOR WHITELEY

Mystery Short Story Collections
Criminally Good Stories Volume 1: 20 Detective Mystery Short Stories
Criminally Good Stories Volume 2: 20 Private Investigator Short Stories
Criminally Good Stories Volume 3: 20 Crime Fiction Short Stories
Criminally Good Stories Volume 4: 20 Science Fiction and Fantasy Mystery Short

Stories
Criminally Good Stories Volume 5: 20
Romantic Suspense Short Stories

Connor Whiteley Starter Collections:
Agents of The Emperor Starter Collection
Bettie English Starter Collection
Matilda Plum Starter Collection
Gay Romance Starter Collection
Way Of The Odyssey Starter Collection
Kendra Detective Fiction Starter Collection

Science Fiction Short Story Collections
Rivetingly Great Stories Volume 1
Rivetingly Great Stories Volume 2
Rivetingly Great Stories Volume 3
Rivetingly Great Stories Volume 4
Rivetingly Great Stories Volume 5

www.ingramcontent.com/pod-product-compliance
Lightning Source LLC
LaVergne TN
LVHW022217200926
848481LV00006B/2005